Twayne's English Authors Series

EDITOR OF THIS VOLUME

Sylvia E. Bowman

Indiana University

John Marston

TEAS 216

JOHN MARSTON

By R. W. INGRAM
The University of British Columbia

TWAYNE PUBLISHERS
A DIVISION OF G. K. HALL & CO., BOSTON

Published in 1978 by Twayne Publishers,
A Division of G. K. Hall & Co.

Printed on permanent/durable acid-free paper and bound
in the United States of America

First Printing

For Neil and John

Library of Congress Cataloging in Publication Data

Ingram, Reginald W   1930-
John Marston.

(Twayne's English authors series ; TEAS 216)
Bibliography: p. 169-77
Includes index.
1. Marston, John, 1575?-1634
Criticism and interpretation.
PR2697.I5   822'.3   78-7504
ISBN 0-8057-6725-8

Contents

About the Author

Reginald W. Ingram was born in Coventry, England on October 3, 1930. He was educated in Coventry. He received his Bachelor of Arts degree in English Language and Literature, and his Master of Arts degree in English at the University of Birmingham, and his Doctor of Philosophy degree in English at the University of London. He has taught on the college level for more than twenty years in the following institutions: Baghdad University, Indiana University, the University of Chicago, and the University of British Columbia.

Dr. Ingram has published articles and reviews in various professional journals on medieval and Tudor drama and on particular playwrights and the use of music in their plays—Marston, Shakespeare, Fletcher, Brome. In recent years he has been working on medieval dramatic entertainments in Coventry and has prepared an edition of the dramatic records of Coventry from 1392 to 1642 which will appear as the third volume in *Records of Early English Drama* (he is a member of the executive editorial board of *REED* which operates out of the University of Toronto). He is currently writing a book on *The Tempest* and the Arts.

Preface

The reaction to John Marston's plays, which began in the late 1590s and has continued ever since, has been well put by Algernon Swinburne:

"The praise and the blame, the admiration and the distaste excited by his works, are equally just, but are seemingly incompatible; the epithets most exactly appropriate to the style of one scene, one page, one speech in a scene or one passage in a speech, are most ludicrously inapplicable to the next. An anthology of such noble and beautiful excerpts might be collected from his plays, that the reader who should make his first acquaintance with this poet through the deceptive means of so flattering an introduction would be justified in supposing that he had fallen in with a tragic dramatist of the very highest order—with a new candidate for a station in the very foremost rank of English poets. And if the evil star which seems generally to have presided over the literary fortunes of John Marston should misguide the student, on first opening a volume of his works, into some such arid or miry tract of wilderness as too frequently deforms the face of his uneven and irregular demesne, the inevitable sense of disappointment and repulsion which must immediately ensue will too probably discourage a casual explorer from any renewal of his research."[1]

T. S. Eliot sensed distinguished qualities in Marston's plays and marked out *Sophonisba* above the rest—"it is austere and economical." Alfred Harbage, on the other hand, reckoned that "any of Marston's plays may be defined as a five-act lapse in good taste." Robert Ornstein calls him "one of the more stable personalities who wrote for the Jacobean stage," while Samuel Schoenbaum, in a famous article, argued his "precarious balance."[2] Today, opinion—a force Marston held in little esteem—is more inclined to appreciate him. The vogue for dark comedy and satire has found in Marston a precursor of much that is proclaimed as modern in today's theater, for old vices have become modern virtues.

My central interest in Marston is his theatricality. He was fascinated by the artifice of the theater, and his vigorously inventive exploration of the art of the theater is what I wish to focus on in this study. The interplay between author, actor, role, and audience; the shifting wonder of stage spectacle; the mingled appeal to eyes and ears at once; the counterpoint of different voices and the movement of people; the fusing of words and music and actions—these dramatic aspects never failed to excite Marston's imagination. He was sensitive to the gulf that yawned between the spectator in the theater and the reader in his home: he continually reminds the reader of his plays that he is reading a drama whose life "consists in action" and "rests much in the actor's voice." I have tried to heed these reminders by treating the plays primarily as theatrical pieces meant to be seen and to be heard. Marston has often been abusively termed "theatrical"; I wish to present him as a theatrical man in the richer sense of the word, as one whose natural gifts found exciting and spontaneous expression on the stage.

It will readily become obvious that I have used the guidebooks to the "wild and irregular demesne" of Marston provided by earlier explorers—A. J. Axelrad, Anthony Caputi, Gustav Cross, Arnold Davenport, R. A. Foakes, Philip Finkelpearl, and G. K. Hunter. None of these sees the landscape with the same eyes, and each suggests different vantage points and takes his own path. Though my path often joins for a while, and sometimes crosses, one of theirs, I can only hope that it generally takes its own course. In fact, my route leaves certain things far off, and others it bypasses altogether. Textual, bibliographical, and source problems are omitted; not all works associated with Marston are discussed; but *Histriomastix* is included because I think that most, if not all, of it is Marston's. *The Insatiate Countess* is excluded because the large part of it is not, I think, by Marston; and, fascinating though some of it is from a dramaturgical point of view, it is very difficult to decide for how much of it Marston should be held responsible. I am sadder at leaving *Eastward Hoe* aside; but since neither the division of its parts between Marston, Ben Jonson, and George Chapman nor the credit for its overall design and progress can be finally decided, I prefer to omit it and to focus attention on Marston's known work. Gustav Cross has argued for the inclusion of *Lust's Dominion* in the canon; and, though merely his appearance as advocate is formidable, I have yet to be convinced that Marston wrote this play.

Marston was a satiric poet before he was a dramatist, and a prolegomenon to any study of his plays is a survey of his nondramatic work together with some indication of his character and impulses to satire. Accordingly, after an introductory chapter that surveys

Marston's life and sketches salient aspects of his character, the next two chapters deal with his verse satires. The fourth chapter moves from them to the plays by tracing the course of his two major literary quarrels. In remaining chapters, the plays are discussed individually, approximately in chronological order. The exact order is not known and I have not paused to argue dating because what I have to say does not depend upon an absolute order of composition. Marston matures in both thought and technique, but his artistic and intellectual maturity does not necessarily exhibit itself in nice gradations from work to work.

R. W. INGRAM

University of British Columbia

Acknowledgments

I wish to express my gratitude to the University of British Columbia, which provided research grants to aid the writing of this book.

Quotations are taken, with permission, from *The Poems of John Marston*, edited by Arnold Davenport (Liverpool University Press, 1961), and from *The Plays of John Marston*, edited by H. Harvey Wood (3 vols. Edinburgh, 1934–39). Neither text is modernized. There is no line numbering in the play text and references are keyed to the volume and page. Quotations from Shakespeare are taken from *The Norton Facsimile of the First Folio*, prepared by Charlton Hinman (New York, 1968), and quotations from Jonson are from the text edited by C. H. Herford and Percy and Evelyn Simpson (11 vols. Oxford, 1925–1952).

I am grateful to the editors of *Music and Letters* and *The Humanities Association Bulletin* (Canada) for permission to use material that originally appeared in their journals.

I should also like to express my gratitude to Sylvia E. Bowman for her patience and invaluable editorial assistance.

Chronology

1575   September 19: John Marston, father of the dramatist, married Marie Guarsi (daughter of an Italian physician who settled in London) at Wardington, near Banbury, the Guarsi family home (Marston owned property in the neighboring village of Cropredy).

1576   October 7: John Marston, the dramatist, christened at Wardington. Probably lived, and went to school in Coventry (no surviving school records mention him) where his father practiced law and was steward of the city, 1588–99 (there is frequent mention of John Marston, Sr., in civic and guild accounts during this period).

1592   February 4: matriculates Brasenose College, Oxford University.

       August 2: entered as member of Middle Temple by his father who was then a reader there.

1594   February 6: graduates Bachelor of Arts.

1595   November 20: resides in the Middle Temple.

1598   *The Metamorphosis of Pigmalions Image and Certaine Satyres.*

       The Scourge of Villanie (second and third editions with additional "Satyra Nova" in 1599).

1599   September 28: Henslowe notes the sum of forty shillings loaned to Marston for an unnamed play. Arguments exist for it being *Robert II, King of Scots*, a lost play in which Jonson and others had a hand, or *Lust's Dominion*.

1599   Father dies: will dated October 24, at Coventry, and proved on November 29. *Histriomastix* (printed for the first time 1610), *Antonio and Mellida* (printed 1602).

1600   *Jacke Drum's Entertainment* (printed 1610).

1601   *Antonio's Revenge* (printed 1602), *What You Will* (printed 1607). Contributed a poem to "Divers Poetical Essays" appended to Robert Chester's *Love's Martyr* (Jonson, Chapman, and Shakespeare also contributed).

1602   November 21: "Jo. Marstone the last Christmas when he daunct with Alderman Mores wives daughter, a Spaniard borne, fell into a strang commendacion of her witt and beauty. When he had done, shee thought to pay him home, and told him she though[t] he was a poet. 'Tis true,' said he, 'for poetes fayne, and lye, and soe dyd I when I commended your beauty, for you are exceeding foule.' " Entry in *The Diary of John Manningham of the Middle Temple 1602–1603* (f.66b).

1603   Prefatory verses to Jonson's *Sejanus.*

1604   Buys a sixth share in management of Children of the Queen's Revels for whom he wrote the rest of his plays. *The Malcontent* for Children of the Queen's Revels then taken over for King's Men (with Induction by Webster). *The Fawne* (?) (printed 1606).

1605   *The Dutch Curtezan* (printed 1605). Collaborated with Jonson and Chapman on *Eastward Hoe*. As a result of some passages insulting to Scots and James I, Jonson and Chapman were imprisoned and possibly Marston also. A letter of Chapman's suggests the offending passages were written by Marston. *Sophonisba* (printed 1606). Presumably marries Mary Wilkes, daughter of William Wilkes, rector of Barford St. Martin in Wiltshire.

1606   July 31: *City Spectacle* performed for James I and his guest, the King of Denmark.

1607   Early in August at or near Ashby de la Zouche in Leicestershire for performance of his *Entertainment of the Dowager-Countess of Darby*. Probably working on *The Insatiate Countess* which was completed by William Barksted and printed in 1613.

1608   June 8: commited to Newgate prison by order of Privy Council; remained there for an undetermined time. Reason for imprisonment not known but supposed due to performance of offensive play (by Marston?) at Blackfriars. In July or August sells his share in Blackfriars.

1609   September 24: ordained deacon in parish church of Stanton Harcourt, Oxfordshire. December 7: granted permission to use Bodleian. December 24: ordained priest in same church.

1610   June 18: listed by Cuthbert Burbage as intended witness and called "John Marston of Barford in the county of wiltes clerk."

1616   August: attacked and robbed of his horse and trappings, sword and some clothes, money and valuables near Knightsbridge, Essex. One Sir George Sandes was charged and acquitted. October 10: became incumbent of Christchurch, Hampshire.

1621   Mother dies: he inherits property in Coventry.

1624   His only son dies in infancy.

1631   September 13: resigns living at Christchurch.

1633   William Sheares issues six plays in a collected edition (*Antonio and Mellida, Antonio's Revenge, What You Will, The Fawne, The Dutch Curtezan, Sophonisba*) apparently without Marston's permission for Sheares was made to withdraw the collection until Marston's name had been removed from it.

1634   June 17: draws up will, too ill to sign so makes mark. June 25: dies at his house in Aldermanbury, London. Buried in Middle Temple under stone with self-chosen epitaph of "Oblivioni Sacrum" (Sacred to oblivion) (Memorial destroyed in air raid during World War II.)

1657   Mary Marston is buried July 4; according to her wish, "by the body of my dear husband."

CHAPTER 1

Life and Character

I "I Am My Selfe, So Is My Poesie"

JOHN Marston's distinctive personality marks all he wrote. From his first appearance in print, in 1598 with *Pigmalion's Image*, his was a personality that commanded attention. Reticence and neutrality have no part in it:

> A partiall praise shall never elevate
> My setled censure, of mine owne esteeme.
> A cankered verdit of malignant Hate
> Shall nere provoke me, worse my selfe to deeme.
> Spight of despight, and rancors villanie,
> I am my selfe, so is my poesie.
> *(The Scourge of Villanie,* To Detraction, 19–24)

This is candid, but Marstonian candor is deceptive: it presents difficulties even as it seems to solve them. Marston was always himself but that self is compounded of contradictions, puzzles, discongruities, and a relish for contrariety and argument.

His vituperative power quickly became his trademark, for the anonymous author of *The Return from Parnassus* (1599–1601) labeled him a "Furor Poeticus" (The Angry Poet):

> A Ruffian in his style
> Withouten bands or garters ornament,
> He quaffes a cup of Frenchmans Helicon,
> Then royster doyster in his oylie tearmes,
> Cutts, thrusts, and foines at whomesoever he meets,
> And stewes about Ram—ally meditations.
> (1.11.269–74: part 2)

If this was notoriety, there was also fame; for Marston is called, on the title page of *Loves Martyr* (1601), one of "the best and chiefest of our moderne writers." A "setled censure" has to take account of both views. Had he been only a blustering literary vagabond like Furor Poeticus, had he been merely a poetaster like the ludicrous Crispinus that Ben Jonson caricatured him as being, he could not have been taken seriously either by his contemporaries then, or by critics since. He attracted the attention of men like Jonson and even, for spells, their friendship and esteem because he was not a mere idle braggart. His conventional response to the criticism he received was to denounce it as the "foule canker of faire vertuous action" (SV, To Detraction, 1); his unconventional response to it was to heed it. He learned from it and, as he rightly claimed, reformed his muse thereby. Such unexpected turns and dualities are the mark of his career. His wildest arguments are usually based on good grounds, his strangest flights often carry him to some place of vantage; his boisterousness is not cheap bullying; no matter how rough or uncontrolled his writing sometimes is, it is the product of a strong mind, not a weak one.

II   Early Life and Education

John Marston was christened on October 7, 1576, at Wardington in Oxfordshire, where the family of his mother, Marie Guarsi, lived. He was probably born there and not, as was long traditionally supposed, at Coventry, some twenty miles to the north, where his father, also John, a distinguished member of the Middle Temple, practiced law and was, from 1588 until his death in 1599, steward of the city. His father's house was in Coventry (it faced onto the marketplace in the city center) and here he was probably raised and educated. It was hoped, or assumed, that he would become a lawyer. In August 1592, he was made a member of the Middle Temple by his father, who was then reader there; and, after graduating from Oxford University, he assumed residence there, shared his father's chambers, and began to study law; but this move was as far as he went in satisfying his father's wishes. On October 24, 1599, when John Marston, Senior made his will, he left the contents of his Middle Temple chambers to his son but "for my lawe bookes beinge a double Corse thereof, I bequeath them to hym that deserveth them not that ys my willfull disobedyent sonne whoe I think will sell them rather than use them although I tooke paynes and had delighte therein god blesse hym and give hym trewe knowledge of hymself and to foregoe his delighte in playes vayne studdyes and fooleryes." The dying father, who deleted these harsh words, resignedly bequeathed his law books "to my sonne wherein I have taken greate paynes with delighte and hoped that my sonne would have proffetted in the studdye of the lawe wherein I bestowed my uttermost indevor but man proposeth and god disposeth."[1]

Although he had no intention of becoming a lawyer, Marston continued to live in the Middle Temple, but there was nothing odd about this arrangement. In the last decade of the sixteenth century, only 15 percent of those who entered the Inns ever practiced law as a profession.[2] Most were there because it was thought that an almost necessary part of education for a man of property was to attain some familiarity with the law. Most of the students were, like Marston, sons of professional men or of the landed gentry.

As a member of the Middle Temple, Marston was one of a relatively close-knit group of literate, cultured, lively men who lived in an atmosphere that was "free-spoken, irreverent, independent."[3] Life there was, by turns, bright and lively or garish and rough. Since the members were being trained to argue, they did so very freely and about any question, whether of law, politics, religion, social mores, or literature. They relished mockery—their annual entertainments relied much upon it—and one of their natural bents was toward satire. Marston, a man with a vigorous and abrasive intellect who was driven by fine ideas and high aspirations which he had yet to refine, needed to argue his opinions; and no more congenial company could have been found. His immediate contemporaries included not only (inevitably) future judges, but political leaders such as John Pym and writers such as John Davies, Henry Wotton, Thomas Overbury, John Ford, and, possibly, John Webster. This company was a nursery for strong minds not weak ones.

III   *Literary Career*

Although one purpose of the Inns of Court was to sharpen the skills of debate in its students, Marston, who never needed encouragement to dispute, was only gradually to learn the difference between speaking freely and speaking without license. In fact, it may be doubted that he ever completely mastered the difference before he quitted the theater. Moreover, the satirists of the 1590s were as quick to attack each other as they were to excoriate society's faults generally; and Marston, who was quicker than most to sense personal slights, waged fierce battles in his verse satires with Joseph Hall, then a brilliant student at Cambridge and later to become Bishop of Exeter and Norwich; and in his plays with Ben Jonson. Eventually, and finally, he chose to dare the more dangerous wrath of James I.

Marston began his writer's career with the unprepossessing *Pigmalion's Image*, which he was soon stridently defending in *Certaine Satyres* (these two were published together in 1598). His satiric vein was expanded in his next collection, *The Scourge of Villanie* (1598, reprinted with an additional satire that continues his attacks on Hall in 1599). He had probably begun to write plays at this time but only turned completely to the stage after the bishops' order against various satiric and erotic poems in the summer of 1599 made the pursuit of verse satire dangerous.

In quick order he wrote *Histriomastix* (1599), *Jacke Drum's Entertainment* (1599–1600), *Antonio and Mellida* (1600), *Antonio's Revenge* (1601), and *What You Will* (1601).[4] The watershed in Marston's brief dramatic career was Jonson's *Poetaster* (1601), for its strictures about his style gave Marston pause for thought. For two years after *Poetaster*, Marston was silent, and then published in 1604 *The Malcontent*, dedicated to Jonson as the first product of a reformed muse. The new friendship lasted a year longer, culminating in the writing of *Eastward Hoe* (1605) together, in which project George Chapman also joined. Some jibes in this play at James I and his Scots resulted in jail for Jonson and Chapman, but not for Marston despite their insinuation that the offensive material was his. The friendship with Jonson cooled again; and Marston, having written commendatory verse for Jonson's Roman tragedy, *Sejanus*, in 1603, published his own attempt in that genre, *Sophonisba* (1605), with a derogatory reference to *Sejanus:* "To transcribe Authors, quote authorities, and translate Latin prose orations into English blank-verse, hath in this subject beene the least aime of my studies."[5]

The Malcontent, The Dutch Curtezan (1605), *The Fawne* (1604), and *Sophonisba* are Marston's last four completed plays and his best work, and the last three were written for the Children of the Queen's Revels and acted in its theater, the Blackfriars, of which Marston had become a shareholder in 1603/1604. *Sophonisba* marks the end of six years' ceaseless theatrical activity by Marston. The works after it that survive include a very short Latin *Spectacle* written for the King of Denmark's visit to London in July 1606, and a masque presented before the Dowager Countess of Derby in July 1607.

Although *The Insatiate Countess* may have been begun about 1607, Marston did not finish it; this may be due to his turning to more formal studies. *The Fawne* and *Sophonisba* are as theatrically exciting as any of his plays, but both are marked by an unusual sobriety and control: Marston indeed went out of his way to stress the pains he had taken with *Sophonisba*. The sense of serious thought rides more naturally and firmly beneath the theatricality in these plays than in his earlier ones. Although Marston always had been concerned about society's and man's behavior, he was seemingly beginning to seek a more direct way to cure them than was offered by staging plays.

When Marston applied for reading privileges at the Bodleian Library in December 1609, he claimed to have been studying philosophy for more than three years; and this claim may have been more than a merely formal one. His tenancy in the Middle Temple had lapsed in 1606, and he surrendered it formally in November of that year. Sometime in 1605 or 1606 he had married Mary, daughter of the Reverend William Wilkes, a favorite chaplain of James I, who held the living of Barford in Wiltshire and who also owned valuable property in Coventry.[6] For eleven years from the time of this marriage until Marston secured the incumbency of Christchurch in Hampshire, Wilkes gave board and lodging to Marston, his wife, and their two servants, for all of which he forgave them payment in his will. During the years 1606–1609, Marston, financially supported by his father-in-law, combined his serious studies, which eventually led him into the church, with a little dramatic writing and with an interest in commercial theater enterprises in ways which are not now clear. What caused him once and for all to abandon the theater for the pulpit can only be conjectured. Little is known of the marriage save that the only child, a son, came late and died in infancy in 1624. Mary Marston died in 1657 and was buried, as she wished, "by the body of my dear husband" in the Temple Church, London.

In March 1608, all London theaters were closed because of two plays, one of which was offensive to the French court (probably *Charles, Duke of Byron* by Chapman), while the other one (possibly *The Fawne*) attacked James, his favorites, and a particular scheme of his for mining in Scotland. James vowed that the perpetrators should "never play more but should first begg their bred and he wold have his vow performed."[7] It is generally assumed that Marston wrote the second play and that, because of it, he was committed to Newgate prison by order of the Privy Council on June 8. It is odd that, having run dangerously foul of James in 1605, Marston should have tempted the royal wrath again; but, if the persuasive arguments that Gonzago in *The Fawne* is a portrait of James are accepted, one might feel that Marston had some particular defiance of James that he was willing to express.[8] It is odder, perhaps, that, if the notorious offense of March 1608 was laid at Marston's door, it was not dealt with until June.

Nonetheless, in the summer of 1608 Marston severed his connections with the theater. He sold his shares in the Blackfriars Theater where the offensive plays had been staged (possibly his punishment was for allowing the performance rather than supplying the material for it), and he wrote no more plays. Nothing more is heard of Marston until his ordination as a deacon in September 1609, and as a priest on Christmas Eve of the same year. One can only conjecture how long he spent in Newgate; why he was released; what part, if any, his father-in-law, as one liked by James, took in the affair; and whether or not his ordination and removal to Barford was part of the settlement. The command of James or his judges may have forced the change sooner than Marston planned, but Marston's inclination for it had existed before the turmoil of summer 1608.

From 1609 until 1631, Marston attended to clerical duties far from London; and the affairs of the stage touched him directly, and briefly, only once more. In 1633, William Sheares published a collection of six of Marston's plays, paid fulsome tribute to the author in a preface, but neglected to seek his prior approval. Marston had the edition withdrawn until all trace of his name had been removed, for his youthful urge to win literary fame had abated with the years. To whatever extent he had come to that "trewe knowledge of hymself" that his father had sought for him, and to whatever extent he had indeed foregone his "delighte in playes vayne studdyes and fooleryes," at the end of his life his "setled censure of owne esteeme" in some ways had not altered. When he died in 1634, he had carved on his tombstone only: *Oblivioni Sacrum*. This phrase was a measured restatement from Marston's *The Scourge of Villanie* that had been dedicated "To Everlasting Oblivion" in 1598. That epilogue was both a young man's defiant gesture as well as a serious comment about literary fame. Marston sought fame, but he did so only on his own hard terms.

CHAPTER 2

Pigmalion's Image: *The Metamorphosis of a Poet*

FOR a young man who sought literary fame in the 1590s, two courses were especially attractive: he could write verse satires as scathing and scurrilous as he dared, or attempt the richly sensuous Ovidian love poem, the epyllion. Curiously enough, it is not clear which of the two courses Marston was following when he wrote his first poem, *Pigmalion's Image* (1598); but his contemporaries believed he had tried and failed to write an Ovidian love poem. It must have been circulated in manuscript or in some form now lost, for the first edition known is that of 1598 when it appeared as the first poem in a small collection of verse: *The Metamorphosis of Pigmalion's Image, and Certaine Satyres*. The first of the *Certaine Satyres*, "The Authour in Prayse of his precedent Poem," is a rampaging defense of *Pigmalion's Image* on the grounds that it is actually a wicked parody of what Marston considered a very distasteful genre.

Whatever the prepublication attacks on the poem, they were deserved. Dull and indecent, the poem amply proved that Marston was temperamentally unsuited to writing in the mode of one who, as he said in a prefatory piece to the poem, "lisp'd like an Amorist." The problem to be resolved is whether or not he was trying so to lisp in *Pigmalion's Image*. Many of his contemporaries thought he was and continued to think so despite his blustering denials. Having failed to divine the poem's satiric intent, his critics were neither comforted nor convinced by Marston's furious explanations; if they had been, he would not have had to return to the question of the poem's genre in *The Scourge of Villanie* (1599).

Pigmalion's Image tells how the sculptor Pigmalion fell so deeply in love with the statue of a woman he had carved that he begged Venus to endow it with life. The poem is lifeless and heartless; its eroticism and sensuality are spurious; Pigmalion's loving admiration of his statue is vulgar ogling; and the later descriptions of lovemaking are as crude as they are cold. Moreover, the imagery is trite; the language is flat and repetitive. "The Authour in Prayse" maintains that the poverty of the verse was deliberate and subtly contrived, for the stanzas

> March rich bedight in warlike equipage:
> Glittering in dawbed lac'd accoustrements,
> And pleasing sutes of loves habiliments.
> Yet puffie as Dutch hose they are within,
> Faint, and white liver'd, as our gallants bin;
> Patch'd like a beggars cloake, and run as sweet
> As doth a tumbrell in the paved street.
>
> (20–26)

In reality, the lines are by no means as cleverly written as this quotation suggests; they are merely very ordinary. The only flickers of life appear when acerbic comments about contemporary affairs stress Pigmalion's actions. The Ovidian lovepoem allowed the narrator to make gravely mocking asides as he told his story; but, although Marston can occasionally manage an equable objectivity— "Loves eyes in viewing never have their fill" (st. 7)—he is usually far too tart, as he is when Pigmalion moves from gazing on his statue to kneeling in adoration before it:

> Looke how the peevish Papists crouch, and kneele
> To some dum Idoll with their offering,
> As if a senceles carved stone could feele
> The ardor of his bootles chattering,
>   So fond he was, and earnest in his sute
>   To his remorsles Image, dum and mute.
>
> (st. 14)

This statement makes rough fun of the Papists, but even rougher fun of Pigmalion and his feeling. The asides can hardly be taken as proof of Marston's satiric intent, for he generally tries to paint a sympathetic portrait of the hero. The usual sharpness of the asides jars the mood of the poem, such as it is. Marston lacks the control for larger comment; and, when he makes the attempt, his own bitterness and lack of sympathy with his theme defeat the intention.

The awareness of a lack of sympathy with the theme of love begins to strengthen into a feeling that Marston is antipathetic to love itself. He describes lust rather than love: in lovemaking he more readily finds beastliness than beauty. He exploits the cheap device of suggesting the action, then pretending in a sniggering fashion that he dare go no further, and finally denouncing the device and condemning those readers whose "gaping eares" he was seeking: "And chaster thoughts, pardon if I doe trip/Or if some loose lines from my pen doe slip" (38). He is willing, however, to let the loose lines slip from his pen because he thinks he will avoid censure by putting an apology for them by their side. After this clumsy trickery, the poem perfunctorily ends in one stanza.

Pigmalion's Image is a confusing poem that strongly suggests a confused writer. Marston is unsure about what he wants to do and how he should do it: he would be the calm narrator of a sensual love story making occasional shrewd comments, but he lacks the technique for the poetry and the maturity for the comments. Underlying everything is his lack of faith in the genre: everything is colored by his irresolution. In defending his poem, he goes to the other extreme and is overly resolute. The thunder and rattle of "The Authour in Prayse" sounds far more like a bad-tempered outburst about falling foul of the critics in his first literary venture than an amused explanation of how well he had fooled them all. He demanded that they should now "tremble at a barking Satyrist." No one was ever to deny that he was "a barking Satyrist" (many a mockery of his manner turned on this favorite canine image of his), but his critics showed little inclination to tremble.

When Marston, returning to the defense of his first poem, asked in *The Scourge of Villanie*, "Yet deem'st that in sad seriousnes I write/Such nastie stuffe as is *Pigmalion*?" (6. 6–7), he evades one of the points at issue: that whether he wrote in "sad seriousnes" or not, he succeeded only in writing "nastie stuffe." Shifting his ground a little, he brashly counters the evasion by arguing that the poem was "lewd stuffe" because he was aiming to catch the large public that had a taste so depraved that this poem was what it sought. A strange defense, it offers no satisfactory explanation about the real purpose served by offering such readers the material they wanted; and there is little wonder that Marston's critics found the work merely "nastie stuffe." Although the poem could not be salvaged, it did persuade Marston that satire was the mode for which he was best suited. Thereafter, he turned seriously to verse satire; but he had written more truly than he perhaps realized in the opening lines of the first of

the *Certaine Satyres:* "I Cannot show in strange proportion, /
Changing my hew like a Camelion." For, although his verse always
was himself, his attempts to play the lisping amorist were bound to
fail, for he was really the "snaphaunce Satyrist."

CHAPTER 3

The Verse Satires: "Quake to Behold a Sharp-Fang'd Satyrist"

I Elizabethan Melancholy: The Malcontent and Satire

NO other satirist's voice can be mistaken for Marston's:

> I Cannot hold, I cannot I indure
> To view a big womb'd foggie clowde immure
> The radiant tresses of the quickning sunne.
> Let Custards quake, my rage must freely runne.
> Preach not the Stoickes patience to me,
> I hate no man, but mens impietie.
> My soule is vext, what power will'th desist?
> Or dares to stop a sharpe fangd Satyrist?
> Who'le coole my rage? who'le stay my itching fist
> But I will plague and torture whom I list?
>
> (SV, 2.1–10)

However, his sentiments were those of a large group of discontent intellectuals called by the Elizabethans "malcontents." The malcontent was disheartened by and disgusted at society; and, though Joseph Hall may have drawn on memories of Marston for the following "Characterisme of Vice," the unflattering traits are typical and not narrowly personal:

"He speakes nothing but *Satyrs* and Libels, and lodgeth no guests in his heart but Rebels. The inconstant and hee agree well in their felicitie, which both place in change: but herein they differ; the inconstant man affects that which will be, the male-content commonly that which was. Finally, he is a querulous curre, whom no horse can passe by without barking at; yea, in deepe silence of night the very moone-shine openeth his clamorous mouth: hee is the wheele of a well-couched fire-worke; that flies out on all sides, not

25

without scorching it selfe. Every eare was long agoe weary of him, and he is now almost weary of himselfe. Give him but a little respit, and he will die alone; of no other death, than others welfare."[1]

Malcontentedness usually was believed in Elizabethan England to be caused by, and sometimes hardly to be separated from, melancholy. As a fashion, melancholy was thought to be an importation from Italy: Elizabethan travelers, impressed by melancholy's being accepted there as "the malady of great minds," adopted the pose; and London soon knew "the disgruntled and seditious traveler" as a social type.[2] The malcontent was most frequently an able man who considered himself to be unjustly overlooked and undervalued by society. In *The Malcontent*, Altofronto is driven to assume the role of Malevole on these grounds. He has the power to endure and the strength to make society recognize him on his own terms. Without these qualities, the malcontent falls to cynicism; and cynic malcontents were seen either sympathetically as gruff barkers with no dangerous bite or as vicious outsiders content to remain as such. The malcontent villain was the man who responded by laying criminal plots and resorting to intrigue and violence. Possibly least offensive of all was the scholar malcontent who was crushed early by too little food and too much study until he lost touch with reality. Lampatho Doria in *What You Will* is Marston's example of such a scholar.

Melancholy could be caused by grief, loss, sorrow, or sometimes by disease. Some people were melancholy by natural inclination: Marston addresses such a man—"stifled with true sense of misery"— in the Prologue to *Antonio's Revenge*. At best, such men were reflective; at worst, apathetic and slothful. Melancholy lovers made up another large group. They were not conspicuously well treated by Marston on the occasions when they appear; Pasquil and Katherine in *Jacke Drum's Entertainment* are representative examples of this group. To all of these must be added those who adopted melancholy as a fashionable pose, fake travelers like Bruto in *Certaine Satyres* (2.127–42), who hoped to be distinctive and different by assuming melancholy's garb.

The fashion of melancholy first becomes noticeable in English life and letters in the 1580s, but no simple explanation describes why the malcontent and his literary mode, satire, became the vogue in the closing years of Elizabeth's reign. Political, spiritual, intellectual, and social unrest combined to encourage the outburst; but only their barest indications can be presented here. One clue lies in the phrase "the closing years of Elizabeth's reign"; for Elizabeth was aging and, although the force of her personality enabled her to keep hold on affairs and to prevent too open a ventilation of grievances caused by monopolies, enclosures, and the ceaseless rise in prices, restiveness nevertheless was apparent and growing. Uncertainty about the succession was not alleviated by her refusal to name her successor outright; plots were laid and thwarted. The whole dangerous business came to a head when Essex made his bungled foray into London in 1601 and paid for his folly with his life. In such an atmosphere, Shakespeare's history plays were not so much nostalgic evocations of a safely distant past as very present reminders of the horrors of civil war. Moreover, England's security from foreign attack was no longer a matter of placid assurance. The great victory over the Armada in 1588 was only one battle in a long weary struggle which had not ended either additional attempts at invasion or yearly fears of another armada.

The political unrest was also accompanied by spiritual and intellectual questioning: "As the sixteenth century grew older the works of more and more speculative writers became better known in England, and speculation was exercised more freely, and with more and more emphasis on man's life in this world."[3] Machiavelli and Montaigne, to name only two of the more important writers whose works were widely read, did not by any means sweep aside all previous patterns of thought, but their ideas and those they begot slowly began to color men's thinking. On a more profound level, they could be said to have influenced an already existent stratum of skepticism and uncertainty which was part of the aftermath of the Reformation in England: "the soul was no longer guarded from God's wrath by a series of shock absorbers or saintly intermediaries; it stood face to face with the Almighty. As we look back in the period we are tempted to ask whether Protestantism . . . did not put more responsibility on human nature than it could stand, so that, for the time being, a reaction was bound to set in."[4] Whatever the cause, the strain was widely felt.

In the ceaseless struggle for power and position, ancient loyalties and ordinary decencies were abandoned. Eager young men from the universities quickly discovered that ability and vigor counted for little without influence in high places. Tamburlaine and Faustus strode magnificently across Christopher Marlowe's stage, but they were romantic distortions of the average bureaucratic politician and the disappointed schoolman. In real life, the politician was the petty

officeholder guarding his miserable area of power while conniving
voraciously to enlarge it; the teacher shrank to the human stature of
the ill-used and discontented intellectual. For the man inclined to
take this jaundiced view—and it was not a wildly unreasonable
one—he seemed to have no other place than that of an outsider. In
some, this bred a sober melancholy; in others, like Marston, a more
passionate reaction was nourished. In such as Marston there was
fanned an anger that grew into hatred, especially of lust which they
marked as the greatest motivator of society's frenzy. On levels of life
where aspirations were ordinary, if not ignoble, the Renaissance
vision of man's realizing his ambitions encouraged men to exhibit the
worst elements of egoism. Upon this sordid aspect of life—the
grubby, brutal, and small-minded striving for selfish ends and selfish
pleasures—the satirists morbidly focused their attention; and in so
doing, they saw themselves as choosing reality over artificiality.

II   *The Satiric Style*

The seriousness with which the satirists took their task demanded
that they think carefully what satire was and how best it should be
written. "The idea that poetic satire had its origin in a dramatic form
distinguished for its viciousness of attack and spoken by rough satyrs
was the basis for nearly all Elizabethan theories of satire."[5] The satyr
was a rough, shaggy wildman who was banished from or who was
turned against society; and he expressed himself, appropriately to his
status and mode of life, in words that were harsh, abrupt, crabbed,
and violent. Other derivations of the term "satire" included one from
an Arabic word meaning "a sword" or "a sharp weapon"; from the
Latin "satur" meaning "satiated"; from the God Saturn whose
subjects are morose and melancholy. Despite the variety of
etymologies, a unity of feeling about the tone and manner of formal
verse satire exists.

For models, satirists took the great Classical satiric writers,
Juvenal, Persius, Martial, and, to a lesser extent, Horace. In a
prefatory note "To those that seeme judiciall perusers" of *The
Scourge of Villanie,* Marston comments: "*Persius* is crabby, because
antient, & his jerkes, (being perticulerly given to private customes of
his time) duskie. *Juvenall* (upon the like occasion) seemes to our
judgement, gloomie. Yet both of them goe a good seemely pace, not
stumbling, shuffling" (18–23). The urbanity and sophistication of
Horace had rather less appeal. Juvenal commanded the greatest

admiration: he gave the satirists their best motto, "difficile est satiram non scribere," paraphrased by Marston as, "Who would not shake a Satyres knottie rod" (SV, 2.38). Juvenal also gave authority for much that was typical of the satirists' style: exuberant language and newly minted words, sudden changes of speaker, abrupt changes of direction, and bewildering shifts of continuity.

The satirists' declaration that they were following Classical models is true to a lesser extent than they believed. A rich native tradition of satire and, to use an older term, "complaint" was available to them. The abundant detail from contemporary life and manners with which the satires are bursting owes more to Medieval English tradition than to the Roman writers. Medieval sermons contain many sharply etched character sketches that gave example and material to the satirists as much as to the dramatists. The countryman had long been used as a tart commentator on everyday life. In the Corpus Christi Cycles the shepherds mulled over their grievances as they tended their flocks by night; Piers Plowman criticized in the same vein; Thomas Nashe's Pierce Peniless carried on the same tradition in the 1590s and marks the transition from countryman to university man as mouthpiece. Marston can rightly claim allegiance to Classical forebears, but he could not deny owing his satiric qualities to his own native tradition as well.

From the English traditions and from the adoption of the wildman figure of the Satyr, the satiric poet thought of himself as assuming a distinct persona or identity when he wrote his satires. Alvin Kernan, who skillfully charts the confusingly contradictory and unpleasant traits associated with this persona in Renaissance satire, has noted that the distinction between the character of the writer and his satiric persona has always been difficult. "It would be strange indeed," says Kernan, "if every author of formal satire from Nashe to George Wither was sadistic, rough, frank, lascivious, fired by envy, subject to melancholy, guilty of the same sins he castigated, and so stupid that he was unable to conceal any of these weaknesses."[6] Marston suffered much from such direct identification; but some, if not most, of his pains were brought upon himself because when he assumes the role of Satyr, he plays it too enthusiastically. The reader is left to decide whether, when the actor is carried away by his role beyond reason, he should blame the nature of the role or that of the actor.

Marston's comments about the satirist's art are forthright and defiantly inconsistent. They are mostly to be found in a truculent letter addressed to "those that seeme judiciall perusers" of his satire

collection entitled, *The Scourge of Villanie*. Some of his inconsisten-
cies arise from his uncertainty about his audience: he divides his
readers into those sensible people who have no need of his satires and
into the scum (his own word for them) who desperately need their
lessons but are incapable of understanding them. For the former,
who are willing to think and ferret out meanings, he would offer
difficulties of interpretation that gave an air of deep learning[7]: but
such things would defeat his ignorant readers. But there are further
difficulties: Marston tells his "judiciall peruser" that he scorns undue
"obscuritie, & harshnes, because they profit no sence" (1–2);
however, there are those who only relish satires that are "palpable
darke, and so rough writ, that the hearing of them read, would set a
mans teeth on edge" (7–9). Nonetheless, for such ignorant readers,
Marston "wrote the first Satyre in some places too obscure, in all
places misliking me" (9–11) and allowed it to be published. "Rough
writ" lines having been condemned, in the fifth satire the reader
learns that "Rude limping lines fits this leud halting age" (SV, 5.18).
In the face of such confusing testimony it is better to heed Marston's
closing remark to his judicious reader—that he knew that there was
"a seemely decorum to be observed, and a peculiar kinde of speech
for a Satyres lips, which I can willinglier conceive, then dare to
prescribe; yet let me have the substance rough, not the shadow"
(28–32)—and turn to the substance of his satires.

III   *The Content and Design of the Satires*

The groundwork of the satires is simple: the world is corrupt and
decayed; lust, greed, lying, hypocrisy, avarice, usury, sexual perversion, and all manner of idiotic fashions and humors predominate.
Roles of good and evil have been reversed, "Lust, is turned into
Chastitie, / And Riot, unto sad *Sobrietie*" (CS, 5.157–58) in a society
of "Marmosets and mumping Apes" and "fained borrowed shapes"
(SV, 9.103–4). "Slight scapes are whipt, but damned deeds are
praised" (CS, 5.138).

His major theme is the widespread crumbling of social ties and the
disgraceful neglect of religion that are chiefly due to "immodest
looseness . . . inundation of luxuriousness, / Fatts all the world with
such grosse beastlines" (SV, 2.105:140–41). When indignation does
not run away with him, his expression of this feeling has a fine, hard
ironic edge:

Fie, fie, I am deceived all thys while,
A mist of errors doth my sence beguile;
I have beene long of all my wits bereaven,
Heaven for hell taking, taking hell for heaven;
Vertue for vice, and vice for vertue still,
Sower for sweet, and good for passing ill.
. . . .
Tis so, tis so; Riot, and Luxurie
Are vertuous, meritorious chastitie:
That which I thought to be damn'd hel-borne pride
Is humble modestie, and naught beside.

(CS, 5.139–52)

This view is tersely summed up thus:

Well plainely thus, *Sleight, Force, are mighty things,*
From which, much, (if not most) earths glory springs.
If Vertues selfe, were clad in humane shape,
Vertue without these, might goe beg and scrape.

(SV, 5.40–43)

Marston illustrates his condemnation in the satires by parading before the eyes of his reader—eyes that are, by turn, astonished, horrified, amused, glazed, saddened or disgusted—a motley procession:

Apparitions,
Ignes fatui, Glowormes, Fictions,
Meteors, Ratts of Nilus, Fantasies,
Colosses, Pictures, Shades, Resemblances,

(SV, 7.13–16)

Marston depicts a pilgrimage relentlessly treading the road to hell: as a reply to his cry of "A man, a man, a kingdome for a man" (SV, 7.1), it is disheartening. The men Marston sees are condemned to a body that makes the demands of the flesh inescapable, but, although these are too often pandered to in lustful excess, the grace of God is always available. Marston does not ask that the demands of the flesh be denied, only that they be heeded and that they be controlled. As this theme is central to the thought of the satires, so it is most dangerous to the furious young poet. Although there are times when Marston can treat the theme of lust without stumbling into indecency (for example, in SV, 8), he is frequently so disturbed by the sexual depravity and hypocrisy he sees before him that he falls into a stridency and a nauseous detail that are self-defeating (as in SV, 5).

He is on generally safer ground when exposing social and literary foibles. His portraits of the fashion-mad, the social climbers, the city-gallants, and those bores who can talk only of their single interest—the fencer whose life and language are all swordsmanship, the theatergoer who is a walking anthology of good things cribbed from plays, the relentless joke-teller—all of these are sharply drawn. When he treats literary topics he is at his worst only when engaged upon the perilous and foredoomed adventure of rescuing *Pigmalion's Image* (SV, 11). When less personally engaged he takes a humorous survey of poetasters and would-be critics, "windie bubbles" which he amusingly pricks. Here he describes those Bottoms who insist on writing down their dreams:

> Another walkes, is lazie, lyes him downe,
> Thinkes, reades, at length some wonted sleep doth crowne
> His new falne lids, dreames, straight tenne pound to one,
> Out steps some Fayery with quick motion,
> And tells him wonders, of some flowrie vale,
> Awakes straight, rubs his eyes, and prints his tale.
>
> (SV, 6.43–48)

He exercises a natural gift for parody when he glances at the inane verses of foppish lovers, as in the following elegy on a lady's monkey:

> *Heere lyeth hee, hee lyeth heere,*
> *that bounc'd, and pitty cryed,*
> *The doore not op'd, fell sicke alas,*
> *alas fell sicke, and dyed.*
>
> (SV, 8.19–22)

A fop's rhapsody to a hairpin reads:

> *Celestiall blisse,*
> *Can heaven grant so rich a grace as this?*
> *Touch it not (by the Lord Sir)) tis divine,*
> *It once beheld her radiant eyes bright shine:*
> *Her haire imbrac'd it, o thrice happie prick*
> *That there was thron'd, and in her haire didst sticke.*

> Kisse, blesse, adore it *Publius,* never linne,
> Some sacred vertue lurketh in the pinne.

(SV, 8.102–09)

Despite his insistence on the darkness of the scene he is forced to depict, Marston does not end his anatomy of society in any hopeless state of mind. His mood is one of resignation and hope rather than optimism, and fits the all too seldom realized intent to write "In serious jest, and jesting seriousnes." The mood carries over into the farewell verses, "To everlasting *Oblivion,*" wherein Marston asks that he and his poetry, "sharpe, yet well meant," shall ". . . sleepe securely free from love or hate, / From which this living, nere can be exempt, / But whilst it breathes will hate and furie tempt" (11–13). In these lines Marston shows that he sees clearly the nature of the temptations to hate and fury which his lesser self could not resist. Only in his last plays would he finally be able to keep his aggressiveness from overpowering his understanding. A temptation recognized has not yet become a temptation overcome, and when it was he could dramatize what he had learned in *The Dutch Curtezan,* and attempt to prove it in his own life by taking up holy orders.

IV *The Achievements of the Satires*

Marston does not rely upon any structural ordering of his satires for their effect. His appeal is founded primarily on their forcefulness and on the emotional coherence of what he says about the world that he sees and is appalled by. The immediate horror so overwhelms him that he can hardly pull himself back to take a broader, more balanced view. Inevitably, he was suspected of being as much fascinated by the sordid as he was repelled by it; and such a reaction is not an uncommon one. Many people come to terms with some frightening or shocking occurence by a frequent rehearsal of it in one form or another, in conversation, in dreams, in thought. An author masters it by imposing an artistic shape and by recollecting it in writing. Marston cannot master his reaction so easily: he writes in the first flush of emotion and throws down his turbulence directly before the embarrassed reader. The literary form he chose did not help him since it encouraged outspokenness and extremity. What saves him is the fundamental rightness of his cause.

Marston's sense of imminent defeat for man's soul was a very real and important subject. Man's capacity for evil confirmed certain of his pessimistic tendencies, but his own immaturity as a thinker and as a writer also blurred his outlook. The ancient and terrible theme of the struggle of the flesh and the spirit is a proper one for a moral writer, but one that demands maturity, tact, and control in the handling, as well as earnestness and passion; and maturity, tact, and wisdom Marston could hardly bring to his task. The earnestness and control proper to Marston's theme are less obvious than his immaturity and tactlessness, but they are present. What solace Marston found in religion is not known, but one may doubt its being placidly benevolent without one's being skeptical in any way about its piety.

The epitaph Marston chose, "Oblivioni Sacrum," underlines the lack of joyful confidence and affirmation in his philosophy and in his religious thinking as they appear in his satires. He rejects any philosophy that excludes God or that proposes a way of life that ignores the presence of the divine spirit. Without God's gift of grace, man is lost; he cannot find grace of his own accord:

> *Sure Grace is infus'd*
> *By divine favour, not by actions us'd.*
> *Which is as permanent as heavens blisse*
> *To them that have it, then no habite is.*
> *Tomorrow,* nay to day, it may be got:
> So please that gracious Power clense thy spot.
> Vice, from privation of that sacred Grace,
> Which God with-drawes, but puts not vice in place.
> Who sayes the sunne is cause of ugly night?
>
> (SV, 4.117–25)

In its most literal interpretation, such thinking would blunt the satirists' purpose by its denial of man's culpability: Marston assumes, however, that man is capable of being worthy of the gift, "it may be got"; and the manner of the getting is the cleansing of pipes which link man's Soul to its heavenly source. Yet, so clogged are these pipes that, Marston at times professes to think that the whole notion of the essential union of man with his God is a dream. The gift of grace rejected and man "disrai'd/Of that fayre jem," he has only "Beasts *sence*, plants *growth,* like being as a stone, / But out alas, our *Cognisance* is gone" (SV, 7.199–202). "Man has the same quality of mere existence as stones have; the same properties of existence and growth as plants; of existence, growth and sensitiveness as animals; but we lack the distinctively human characteristic of *understand-*

ing."[8] The gift of grace is God's, but man is at liberty to reject or prove himself unworthy of the offer. One way of rejection is to substitute the false chimeras of "Opinion" for heavenly thoughts and right thinking. Reason is given man: it is his "intellectuall," a divine spark of the flame by which he should live; but it is easily robbed of its "bright glosse" by "infeebling ryot." Man makes his body, a "smoakie house of mortall clay," derelict by placing it in the hands of "his dungie, brutish, sensual will." The result is that the soul must slink unnoticed away (SV 8.185 ff.).

All too often Marston fails poetically because his indignation at the decay of man makes his poetry a similarly poor residence for serious thought and earnest pleas. At his worst, he luridly announces himself as one ploughing up

> The hidden entrailes of ranke villanie.
> Tearing the vaile from damn'd Impietie.
> Quake guzzell dogs, that live on putrid slime,
> Skud from the lashes of my yerking rime
>> (Proemium in librum primum, 1.17–20)

The excesses of his "yerking rime" and the incoherence of his "rude limping lines" quickly won him a lasting notoriety; and his noisy defense of them only further mars what is already spoiled while, at the same time, diverting attention from the poetry he best deserves to be remembered by. He chose to be a poet as well as a satirist. As a satirist he insisted that material took precedence over manner; possibly he feared that literary criticism might dismiss his poetry, and with it, his urgent message. But he is a poet, and his insistence upon what he had to say should not blind us, as it never blinded him, to the way in which he tried to say it. The witty parodies quoted earlier attest to his keen ear: his material was always important, but when the subject is grave, and when he writes with forceful control, his words demand attention both as thought and as poetry:

> Snib'd by his baser parts, that now poore *Soule*,
> (Thus pesanted to each lewd thoughts controule)
> Hath lost all hart, bearing all injuries,
> The utmost spight, and rank'st indignities
> With forced willingnes. Taking great joy
> If you will daine his faculties imploy
> But in the mean'st ingenious qualitie.
> (How proude he'le be of any dignitie?)

> Put it to musick, dauncing, fencing schoole,
> Lord how I laugh to heare the pretty foole
> How it will prate, his tongue shall never lie,
> But still discourse of his spruce qualitie;
> Egging his maister to proceed from this,
> And get the substance of celestiall blisse.
> His Lord straight calls his parliament of sence,
> But still the sensuall have preheminence.
> The poore soules better part so feeble is,
> So cold and dead is his *Synderisis*,
> *That shadowes by odde chaunce somtimes are got,*
> *But o the substance is respected not.*
>
>   (SV 11.219–38)

The conclusion is neither pessimistic nor optimistic; the soul lives, but it is weak; despair does not triumph; and the end is jesting seriousness and resignation. This quiet and uneasily hopeful assertion of man's chance for final salvation can seem inconsistent with the general impact of the satires. Their rage and fury, the ghastly images which they throw on the reader, their vision of degradation and loss might seem to demand an equally savage summation. Yet, after the tempest the desolation may hint at renewal. The occasional achievement of an impartial even-temperedness only marks more insistently the too customary harsh irascibility.

In presenting his case, Marston does not discriminate skillfully among his abundant evidence; and much that is handled awkwardly is presented in such a way that it alienates sympathetic hearers and blunts the poet's own good points. His anxiety and impetuosity lead him to shout where he should speak forcefully. The style is at times so turbulent and irritating that the explanation of deliberation cannot redeem it. Honesty makes Marston self-critical; but his fear of being misunderstood, which is allied to a certainty of his own fundamental rightness, makes him, as yet, contemptuous of criticism. He confesses faults truculently and admits humbleness arrogantly. He is so fierce in his exposure of corruption that the manner attracts more attention than the material.

In brief, Marston combines the faults and virtues of immaturity in a mixture thickened by his undoubted talents and his own passionately sensitive nature. He unites an urgent desire to expose evil, to correct mankind, and to express himself forcefully with the drawbacks of impatience, inexperience, and an unsure knowledge of his world. A natural inclination to passion and fiery temper is exacerbated by his chosen material and methods, his uncertainty, and his suspicions of how the public and his fellow writers will react to him. He mixes good and bad means and ends together by rendering to God and to Caesar without adequately discriminating between them. He emerges as a frighteningly determined young man, the nervous and overraucous voice of his group; but he is representative of them and of the mood of the time. His apprehension of the power of words and of language is evident; his style is as yet uncontrolled, but it is urgent with life. A final judgment at this stage in his career might be—and it is one that would have sent him into a rage—that he is neither a failure nor a resounding success but "a very promising writer who should be watched."

CHAPTER 4

The Quarrels with Hall and Jonson

I The Quarrel with Hall

MARSTON thought that he was his own sufficient critic: "Hee
that thinks worse of my rimes then my selfe, I scorne him, for
he cannot, he that thinks better, is a foole" (SV, Judiciall perusers,
35–37). Of those that did think worse, the leader in Marston's
estimation, was Joseph Hall; and no one was more vituperatively
scorned by Marston than the future Bishop of Exeter and Norwich.
Hall, two years older than Marston, published his first satires in 1597:
He announced them with an authoritative but unfounded claim:

> I First adventure, with fool-hardie might
> To tread the steps of perilous despight:
> I first adventure: follow me who list,
> And be the second English Satyrist.
>
> (VIRG, Pro 1, 1–4)

They were entitled *Virgidemiarum,* meaning "a harvest of rods," and
comprised six books of satires. It was the first three books that were
published in 1597: they were "Tooth-lesse Satyrs" dealing, in the
fashion of Juvenal, with poetical, academic, and moral matters. One
year later, three more books "of byting Satyres" appeared that were
more Juvenalian in their daunting obscurity and in their attacks on
persons rather than on types.

The first thing to notice about the quarrel between Hall and
Marston is the small part that Hall took in it. When Marston is one of
the adversaries, however, the adage that it takes two to make a
quarrel loses some of its force. The original cause of the dissension
between the two satirists can only be guessed; although nothing in
Virgidemiae points directly or indirectly to Marston, he may have
assumed that *Pigmalion's Image* was one of the lascivious poems

38

attacked by Hall. Moreover, Hall's provocative claim that he was the first satirist (worsened by his being from Cambridge—"luskish Athens") may have irked Marston. To seek solid grounds for the argument may be needless endeavor, for Marston himself would not have needed any. He did not scruple to abuse Hall on any basis, from the meanest sneers about Hall's early poverty to a wholesale denunciation of his critical faculties. Marston's most ferocious attack is launched in "Reactio," fourth of *Certaine Satyres,* where Hall appears as:

> Vaine envious detractor from the good
> What *Cynicke* spirit rageth in thy blood?
> Cannot a poore mistaken title scape
> But thou must that into thy Tumbrell scrape?
> Cannot some lewd, immodest beastlines
> Lurke, and lie hid in just forgetfulnes,
> But *Grillus* subtile-smelling swinish snout
> Must sent, and grunt, and needes will finde it out?
>
> (CS, 4.25–32)

Marston sets himself up as the defender of all that is decent in the English character against the envious attacks of Hall. Elsewhere, however, readers are assured that Hall's dangerous tendencies are thwarted by the impenetrable obscurity of his writing:

> O darknes palpable! Egipts black night!
> My wit is stricken blind, hath lost his sight.
> My shins are broke, with groping for some sence
> To know to what his words have reference.
>
> (CS, 2.21–24)

Despite the savagery of his attacks, Marston ends "Reactio" with the unexpected invitation:

> Eate not thy dam, but laugh and sport with me
> At strangers follies with a merry glee.
>
> (CS, 4.167–68)

Hall was given little time to accept this invitation. In less than four months, *The Scourge of Villanie* was registered in which Marston returned to the attack. Hall's only known reply to this frontal assault is an epigram:

> I Ask'd Phisitions what theyr counsell was
> For a mad dogge, or for a mankind Asse?
> They told mee though there were confections store,
> Of Poppy-seede, and soveraine Hellebore,
> The dog was best cured by cutting & *kinsing,   *Mark the
> The Asse must be kindly whipped for winsing.   witty
> Nowe then S.K. I little passe   allusion
> Whether thou be a mad dog, or a mankind Asse.   to my name.
> (SV, 10.50–57)

Since Marston had used the pen name of Signior Kinsayder, Hall's use of the initials "S.K." and his punning allusion in the word "kinsing" refer to Marston. The exact meaning of "kinsing" is not known, but it probably has to do with docking the dog's tail or with castrating the dog (with a pun on marstone). Not a notably trenchant epigram, it is to the point. Hall had it inserted in those copies of *Pigmalion's Image* to be found in Cambridge (presumably an earlier edition of the poem of which no copies now remain).

Marston replied furiously to Hall in "Satyra Nova," which he inserted into the second edition of *The Scourge of Villanie* (1599). Ironically, Hall's epigram is saved from oblivion because Marston reprinted it in this satire which depicts Hall, on his dunghill, as a "stinking Scavenger," a "brother of hypocrisie," and a "nittie pedant" whose crimes are compounded by his popularity.

> Shame to Opinion, that perfumes his dung,
> And streweth flowers rotten bones among,
> Jugling Opinion, thou inchaunting witch,
> Paint not a rotten post with colours rich.
>
> (63–66)

Hall kept silent and let Marston's outbursts support his own epigrammatic judgment. But Marston had also spoken his last word:

> From a sickly bed,
> And from a moodie minde distempered,
> I vomit foorth my love, now turn'd to hate
> Scorning the honour of a Poets state.
>
> (73–76)

The main combatants now withdrew, but they let others continue their battle.

II   *The Quarrel Continues Without Hall or Marston*

The quarrel attracted attention, and supporters were found for both sides. Francis Meres thought such quarreling all to the good: "As that ship is endaungered, where all leane to one side, but is in safetie, one leaning one way, and another another way: so the dissensions of Poets among themselves, doth make them, that they lesse infect their readers. And for this purpose our Satyrists, *Hall, the Author of Pigmalion's Image, and certaine Satyres, Rankins,* and such others, are very profitable."[1] This generous view of the matter was not shared by the authorities, nor is it very often found in the dissident poets themselves.

Everard Guilpin, the "very friend, maister E. G." to whom Marston had dedicated "Satyra Nova," was the first to rally to Marston's support, in his *Skialetheia* (1598). In 1599, John Weever, in one of a set of dull epigrams, linked Marston with Jonson and likened Marston's poetic manner to Horace's. He soon repented this judgment; and, in "A Prophesie of this present yeare 1600," he nicked Marston in his own robust manner by mocking his extravagant language and overworked images and by calling him a "wasp-stung Satyrist" driven by "rigorous envy-kindled rage" (6, 16): "What beastlinesse by others you have showne,/Such by your selves tis thought that you have knowne" (152–53). The next contribution to the affray, *The Whipping of the Satyre* (author unknown, 1601), attacks Marston, Jonson, and Guilpin as three of a kind. The prefatory letter charges Marston: "you gathered up mens vices, as though they had been Strawberries, and pickt away their vertues, as they had beene but the stalkes . . . if a man should blazon you aright, hee must make your tongue passant: your anger rampant: and your malice couchant" (93–105). Marston's style receives comment that is as notable for its pertinence as for its outrageous puns:

> Your Readers tongue as every leafe doth tyre:
> Then for a bayte of fresher breath doth stay,
> Each lyne he thinks a lane, and doth desire,
> It were as playne as Dunstable high way;
> When I dare speake it, at the best mans table,
> You deale as playne as any Dunse is able.
>
> . . . .
>
> Hard-hearted Scribe, seeke not with lawlesse pen,
> To crucifie the sonnes, but sinnes of men.
>
> (289–348)

The poem summarizes the major charges against Marston and his satires as foul, uncontrolled speech; indiscriminate attack; indecency; and personal viciousness.

Despite this harsh verdict, Marston was still seen by some as a defender of the faith. In *The Whipper of the Satyre his pennance in a white Sheete: or, The Beadles Confutation* (1601), possibly by Guilpin, the author argues that it is better for man to suffer the slings and arrows of outrageous satirists on earth than to suffer eternally in hellfire or, if beyond salvation, to begin the hellish suffering on earth. The "friendly Satyrist" is urged to continue his good work with a faith that calls for the blind eye as well as the deaf ear:

> Meane time, good *Satyre* to thy wonted traine,
> As yet there are no lettes to hinder thee:
> Thy touching quill with a sweete mooving straine,
> Sings to the soule a blessed lullabie:
>   Thy lines beget a tymerous feare in all,
>   And that same feare deepe thoughts angellicall.
>
> (241–46)

Nicholas Breton, who played the peacemaker's role in *No Whippinge, nor trippinge: but a kinde friendly Snippinge* (1601), admonishes the contestants to write religious poetry if they had to write poetry at all and to discuss constructively and privately each other's faults. Amid an abundance of pleasing animal lore and old proverbs, he optimistically rests his case on the plea: "Play with mee; but hurt me not: and jest with me; but disgrace me not."

III   *Lets to Hinder a Satirist*

To tell the "good Satyre" Marston that "there are no lettes to hinder thee" was to ignore an order made by the Archbishop of Canterbury and the Bishop of London on June 1, 1599, which demanded that certain erotic poems and satires be burned. This action was not taken because of any particular book but because the number of such offensive books circulating was so large as to be a danger. There was nothing especially unsettling to the state in Marston's quarrel with Hall or in Nashe's with Harvey, but the accumulation of such arguments, the bad temper they displayed, and the probing satirical spirit they encouraged had begun to mount to alarming proportions. More importantly, the satirists did not restrict themselves to personal literary disagreements but turned their anger and critical temper against society at large. They shrouded their vision of contemporary life with Classical settings and names; but their readers, who were not deceived, happily played the popular and fascinating game of guessing the contemporary identity of places and persons.

For the satirists' own safety, such writers about people they knew did not wait for the game to begin before declaring it an improper one. Marston's letter "To him that hath perused me" at the end of *The Scourge of Villanie* is typical of these disclaimers:

> . . . I feare me, I shall be much, much, injuried by two sorts of readers: the one being ignorant, not knowing the nature of a Satyre, (which is under fained private names, to note generall vices,) will needes wrest each fayned name to a private unfained person. The other too subtile, bearing a private malice to some greater personage then hee dare in his owne person seeme to maligne, will strive by a forced application of my generall reproofes to broach his private hatred. Then the which I know not a greater injury can be offered to a Satyrist. . . . If any one (forced with his owne guilt) will turne it home and say *Tis I*, I cannot hinder him. Neyther doe I injure him.   (5–24)

This traditional plea is "if the cap fits, wear it." Some important heads, however, felt it to be safer if there were no such caps available for the fitting. In fact, the satires came too close to being a kind of scandalous contemporary history; and Sir Walter Raleigh, in his role of historian, tersely stated the problems and dangers involved in writing contemporary history: "Whosoever in writing a modern History shall follow Truth too near the heels, it may haply strike out his teeth. There is no Mistres or Guide that hath led her followers and Servants into greater miseries."[2] Raleigh's metaphor about truth striking out the teeth of her too-close followers proved to be an apt one for the writers of biting satires. The order of June 1, 1599, though it pulled some teeth, did not cure the urge to bite and snarl.

IV *The Quarrel with Jonson and the War of the Theaters*

Marston, who took the clerical hint, turned to playwriting (indeed, it is probable that he did not wait for it); but, though he tempered his vigorous polemicism a little, the satirist's old bogey of being misunderstood by his readers ironically caught him in an unexpected manner as he quickly fell into a quarrel with Jonson. His good intention had been to compliment Jonson in the character of Chrisoganus, a strong-willed corrector of society's faults, in his first play, *Histriomastix;* but Marston's certain clumsiness of delineation marred Chrisoganus's character with unkind hints of caricature. Such indirections began a quarrel that was a major campaign in the theatrical warfare of 1599–1601.

In the broadest terms, the warfare consisted of competition between rival theaters for audience and income spiced by personal vendettas between individual playwrights. Much of the skirmishing was never reported because it took the form of exchanges behind the scenes in greenrooms, in taverns, and in private rooms that, were they known today, might explain many disputed interpretations of what caused or increased such disputes. For example, the purge that Shakespeare gave Jonson was well enough known to the audience of the anonymous *The Return from Parnassus* for people to need only a reference so casual that it defeats critics today. Naturally, Shakespeare as a professional man of the theater was affected by the theatrical war and his well-known comment upon one aspect of it in *Hamlet* provides a useful introduction to the part played in it by Jonson and Marston. Rosencrantz, talking of the sudden popularity of the Boys' companies, remarks that they have "so be-ratled the common Stages (so they call them) that many wearing Rapiers, are affraide of Goose-quils, and dare scarse come thither . . . . . Faith there ha's bene much to do on both sides: and the Nation holds it no sinne, to tarre them to Controversie. There was for a while, no mony bid for argument, unlesse the Poet and the Player went to Cuffes in the Question" (2.2.1389–1403). Theater owners held it no sin to encourage the controversy because it was good box office; the public, denied one form of argument and satire by the bishops' order, was delighted with the compensatory offerings of such lively disputants as Marston and Jonson. Indeed, two men more likely to go to cuffs about a question would have been hard to find. After some carping remarks about Marston's plays, Jonson told Drummond that "he had many quarrells with Marston, beat him & took his Pistol from him" (H&S 1.140). Marston and Jonson were so alike in some respects and yet so naturally at odds in others that they were bound to clash. Even the unanimity of their desire to purge and correct society by means of satiric drama was not sufficient to overcome their temperamental incompatibility.

Both were proud and irascible men. Jonson, in particular, was inclined to view himself as the master who alone culitvated the proper approach to literature and the stage in a time when his fellows, not excepting Shakespeare, were pandering to popular tastes and abusing their high vocation. Jonson admitted disciples rather than friends; and Marston, much as he admired Jonson, was not cut out to be a humble disciple. Furthermore, Jonson, in his role of idealist and scholar, could hardly relish the assumption of natural partnership between his own Classical rigor and Marston's wild fervor and unlearned carelessness.

V Staging Quarrels: 'Real' People in Plays

Before tracing the history of the quarrel from a mere flicking at mannerisms to the full-scale confrontation of *Poetaster* and *Satiromastix*, two points concerning satirical method in the theater need to be made. In order to do so, an incident from the quarrel is used as an example. In Jonson's *Cynthia's Revels* (1600), there are two characters called Hedon and Anaides:

> The one, a light voluptuous reveller,
> The other a strange arrogating puffe,
> Both impudent, and ignorant inough;
> That talke (as they are wont) not as I merit:
> Traduce by custome, as most dogges doe barke,
> Doe nothing out of judgement, but disease,
> Speake ill, because they never could speake well.
>
> (3.3.25–31)

Although, in a general way, reminiscent of contemporary criticism of Marston as verse satirist, the statement might equally apply to verse satirists generally: there seems to be nothing in the lines here, or elsewhere in the play, that especially suggests Marston, or, for that matter, Thomas Dekker. In *Satiromastix*, the first three of the above lines are quoted, however; and Dekker makes it clear that he thinks that Jonson wrote them with Marston and himself in mind. As a result of this charge of Dekker's, the characters have been closely studied; and, while some critics support Dekker, others suggest that he is mustering retroactive charges against Jonson to justify his own attacks. It must not be assumed, however, that Dekker can only be right if Hedon and Anaides are direct impersonations of Marston and himself. Close imitation of this kind was not intended (except possibly in exceptional cases like *Poetaster* and *Satiromastix*).

When a type or a particular individual was satirized, only one or two personal traits needed to be displayed by the stage character, and those did not need to be presented consistently for the likeness to be

pointed. If, on occasion, the reaction to Hedon is, "That sounds like
Marston," or, "That reminds one of Marston," the job has been done.
An audience could notice such touches without being perturbed that
no total identity exists between the stage character and the living
person he recalls.

The second point to be borne in mind is that, even if close
examination of the text produces nothing to support Dekker's charge,
the denial is being made by a later reader of the play and not by a
witness of its performance. The theater is peculiarly suited to satirize
a person without necessarily giving any clear indication of it in the
text of the play. On the stage, a physical mannerism, a trick of gait, a
gesture with the hand, a manner of talking, an unusual inflection or
pronunciation can be quite enough to direct attention to a comparison
with a living person. "Let us go forward together" is a neutral phrase
until delivered in Churchillian tones.

Such considerations must not allow the doors to be flung wide to all
conjecture on the dubious grounds of what could have been done
with seemingly innocent lines; but, when dealing with special
matters such as the poetomachia, they do encourage belief in
Dekker's assertion. Attacks may well have been looked for on both
sides—Marston's clumsiness in framing the character of Chrisoganus
would not have been helped by the boy actor effecting a parody of
Jonson's manner rather than a glancing copy of it—but looking for
them does not mean they were never there to be found. Hedon
played with red hair would have been enough to point at Marston's
person.[3]

That Jonson and Marston quarreled (and that others were variously
embroiled) is well known. In tracing the quarrel here, a more definite
interpretation is offered than every single item of evidence can
positively bear; for some of the jibes are as much at things Jonsonian
or Marstonian as at those men individually. But, since the existence
of the personal quarrel lends the color of particularity to them, the
history of this quarrel is seen in the simplified terms of Jonson versus
Marston for the sake of clarity.

VI *The First Exchanges*

Marston's Chrisoganus in *Histriomastix* begins as a sort of lesser
Faustus who discourses about the definitions of true knowledge and
who arranges a lecture series about the mysteries of astronomy for a
quartet of lawyers and merchants. However, their zeal for learning

soon withers amid ease and plenty and Chrisoganus is dismissed. He suffers a further blow to his self-esteem when the players reject a play which he has written. He is driven to malcontentedness and rails on popular taste:

> Write on, crie on, yawle to the common sort
> Of thickskin'd auditours: such rotten stuffs,
> More fit to fill the paunch of Esquiline,
> Then feed the hearings of judiciall eares,
> Yee shades tryumphe, while foggy Ignorance
> Clouds bright *Apollos* beauty.
>
> (3.273-4)

The satiric themes are familiar to both Jonson and Marston, but not only is Jonson's manner poorly imitated, but the raucous voice of Marston keeps breaking through. The portrait is obviously not meant as mockery, for Marston supports Chrisoganus's views and sets him in stoic triumph at the end of the play. Nonetheless, admiration for the finer parts of Chrisoganus's character is marred by the smiles of amusement his language invites.

Jonson was seemingly more irritated than insulted when, in *Every Man Out of His Humour* (1599), he replied on behalf of the public players of the Globe to Marston's attack, which was delivered from the private theater of Pauls' Boys. Marston had delivered, through Chrisoganus, a diatribe against the presumption of player-poets:

> O age when every Scriveners boy shall dippe
> Prophaning quills into Thessaliaes Spring,
> When every artist prentice that hath read
> The pleasant pantry of conceipts, shall dare,
> To write as confident as *Hercules*.
>
> (3.274)

Jonson replies in exactly similar terms; but, by inference, he transfers the opprobrium to writers such as Marston:

> O, how I hate the monstrousness of time,
> When every servile imitating spirit,
> (Plagu'd with an itching leprosie of wit)
> In a meere halting fury, strives to fling
> His ulc'rous body in the *Thespian* spring,
> And streight leap's forth a Poet!
>
> (Induc. 66–71)

If it were left to Marston to choose whether he saw himself as one of
those who licked up every idle vanity, no such margin for error was
left in Jonson's more direct but still casual reply to him in the fustian
spoken by the coxcomb, Clove, to impress some gallants:

Clove: Now, sir, whereas the *Ingenuitie* of the time, and the soules *Synderisis*
are but *Embrions* in nature, added to the panch of *Esquiline*, and the
Inter-vallum of the *Zodiack*, besides the *Eclipticke line* being *opticke*, and
not *mentall*, but by the *contemplative* & *theoricke* part thereof, doth
demonstrate, to us, the *vegetable circumference*, and the *ventositie* of the
Tropicks, and whereas our *intellectuall*, or *mincing capreall* (according to the
Metaphisicks) as you may reade in Plato's *Histriomastix* . . . You conceive
me, sir?
Orange: O lord, sir.
Clove: Then coming to the pretty *Animall*, as *Reason long since is fled to
animals*, you know, or indeed for the more *modellizing*, or *enamelling*, or
rather *diamondizing* of your *subject*, you shall perceive the *Hypothesis*, or
Galaxia. . .
Let us turne to our former discourse, for they mark us not.   (3.4.21–40)

Very few of the words ridiculed here can be found in Marston's works,
but the passage as a whole is unmistakably aimed at him. What
matters most is that Marston recognized the sound of his own voice
and assumed Clove was meant for himself. He was little given to
praise, and to receive in return for his act of homage in *Histriomastix*
this brusque treatment from Jonson, one of the "quick sighted
censurers" for whose approval he hoped, hurt him and stung him to
action.

If Jonson had been more concerned with Marstonism than with
Marston himself in Clove's slight speeches, Marston, in *Jacke Drum's
Entertainment*, took aim more directly at Jonson in his characterization of Brabant Sr.; he might have even turned one of Jonson's own
boasts about his sexual prowess against him. Jonson was always too
appreciative of his own worth for his fellow writers' liking: Dekker
castigated his behavior at the theater during performances of his own
plays when he sat making "vile and bad faces at everie lyne" and
drawing attention to himself in every way (*Satiromastix*, 5.2.298 ff.).
Brabant, Sr. loves good wits as companions because, as he modestly
remarks, "mine owne is not unfortunate" (3.194). He is, as Planet
observes, like a mechanical organ, "you need not play upon him,
heele make musicke of himselfe, and hee bee once set going" (3.209).
When Brabant, Sr. and Puffe indulge in an exchange of asinine

compliments, masterminded as it were by Brabant, Sr. who loves to exploit others' weaknesses, Marston returns obliquely the charge of speaking fustian: "By the Lord fustian, now I understand it: complement is as much as fustian" (3.209).

Marston's most direct attack on Jonson's lordly assumption of the role of natural critic of his fellow writers is contained, however, in a short scene in act 4. When Planet and the Brabant brothers enter and begin to talk about contemporary writers, Marston begins with himself as the author of *Antonio and Mellida*:

Bra. Jr.: Brother how like you of our moderne witts? How like you the new Poet *Mellidus?*
Bra. Sr.: A slight bubling spirit, a Corke, a Huske.
Pla.: How like you *Musus* fashion in his carriage?
Bra. Sr.: O filthily, he is as blunt as *Pawles.*
Bra. Jr.: What thinke you of the Lines of Decius? Writes he not good cordiall sappie stile?
Bra. Sr.: A surreinde Jaded wit, but a rubbes on.
Pla: *Brabant* thou art like a paire of Ballance, Thou wayest all saving thy selfe.
Bra. Sr.: Good faith, troth is, they are all Apes & gulls, Vile imitating spirits, dry heathy Turffes.   (3.221)

Brabant senior's contemptuous criticism is answered by Planet:

> . . . I do hate these bumbaste wits,
> That are puft up with arrogant conceit
> Of their owne worth, as if *Omnipotence*
> Had hoysed them to such unequald height,
> That they survaide our spirits with an eye
> Only create to censure from above,
> When good soules they do nothing but reprove.
>
> (3.229)

Planet makes this comment on hearing that there is high hope that Brabant, Sr. has been caught in a jest of his own making. In Brabant, Sr.'s own words: "I to gull the Foole, have brought him to my wife, as to a loose lascivious Curtezan, she being a meer straunger to the Jest, and there some three houres ago left him." (3.239). Wife and fool make the joke a reality, and thus Brabant, Sr. works his own cuckoldry. Marston had often inveighed bitterly against those who sold their wives for gain, but he now uses the device as comedy. In Jonson's conversations with Drummond, the brief recital of the

history of the stage quarrel with Marston is followed immediately by
anecdotes of Jonson's "venerie":

. . . in his youth given to Venerie, he thought the use of a maide, nothing in
comparison to ye wantoness of a wyfe & would never have ane other Mistress.
he said two accidents strange befell him one that a man made his own wyfe to
Court him, whom he enjoyed two yeares erre he knew of it & one day finding
them by chance Was passingly delighted with it.   (Jonson, 1.140)

We cannot tell whether this incident dates from that part of Jonson's
life prior to 1600 or not; but, if it does, it is likely that it formed part of
his raconteur's repertoire and that Marston, knowing it, used it in his
play. This is conjecture, but as least the coincidence of the stories is
worth noting, as is the fact that, if the sequence of Drummond's
recital follows that of Jonson's own conversation, talking about
Marston led directly into that story.[4]

Whatever elements of Jonson's life may lie behind the character of
Brabant, Sr., there was enough of his characteristic behavior in the
work to point the resemblance at him. In *Cynthia's Revels*, Jonson
killed two birds with one stone: he partially repaid Marston for
Brabant, Sr., as well as answering Dekker for some unknown offense.
Hedon and Anaides were sufficiently recognizable targets for their
victims to know them, and the tempo of the quarrel considerably
increased at this point.

Cynthia's Revels was performed late in 1600 at the Blackfriars and
at Court on January 6, 1601. *Poetaster* was performed early in 1601
and was presumably written during the autumn and winter of 1600 as
Jonson wrote the play in fifteen weeks, extraordinarily little time for
him. This haste was forced upon him by the knowledge that Dekker
was preparing a full-scale attack. At about the same time, but
probably a little before Jonson's *Poetaster* came out in 1602, Marston
probably wrote *What You Will*. To this bustle of playwriting,
Dekker's *Satiromastix* made the climax in the late summer of the
same year, for it reflected Jonson's background and characteristics
that were well known in 1601.

What You Will is another such compendium of theatrical variety as
was *Jacke Drum's Entertainment:* the characters of Planet and
Brabant, Sr. are the models of the Quadratus and Lampatho Doria in
the later play. Once again, neither is a straightforward impersonation
of either Marston himself or Jonson, but each represents instead the
type of critic which Marston thought he and Jonson represented.
Like Jonson, who had used the Induction to *Every Man Out of His*

Humour to talk about the purpose and means of what he called "comicall satyre," Marston uses the Induction to *What You Will* to offer a dissenting opinion. Atticus, Doricus, and Phylomuse enter the stage to sit talking of different critics' approaches to plays. Phylomuse angrily denies that the author need concern himself with the audience's opinions, but Doricus interrupts to disagree that one should

> crack rude skorne even on the very face
> Of better audience. . . . .
> *Musike and Poetry* were first approv'd
> By common scence; and that which pleased most,
> Held most allowed passe: not rules of Art
> Were shapt to pleasure, not pleasure to your rules.
> Thinke you if that his sceanes tooke stampe in mint
> Of three or foure deem'd most juditious,
> It must inforce the world to currant them?
> That you must spit defiance on dislike?
>
> (2.232–33)

Marston generously assumes a judicial audience for the purpose of his argument, but that hardly weakens what he has to say and it balances the contempt for the audience which Asper had shown. The result of Doricus's castigation is that Phylomuse abandons his bitterness.

In the main body of the play less about Jonson the man than about his attitude is attacked. Of course, some shafts are directed at Jonson's more vulnerable personal foibles:

> Doth he but speake, *O tones* of heaven it selfe,
> Doth he once write, *O Jesu* admirable
> Cryes out *Symplicius:* then *Lampatho* spittes,
> And sayes faith 'tis good.
>
> (2.246)

Lampatho is daunted continually by Quadratus until he flies into wild flights of invective, whereupon he is roundly charged with railing out of spite and self-pitying envy. Lampatho is of that breed, accuses Quadratus, who make any behavior whatsoever a particular quirk of character and something to be derided: "A man can skarce put on a tuckt up cap, /A button'd frizado sute, skarce eate good meate, / *Anchoves, caviare,* but hee's *Satyred*" (2.250). He develops a clever defense of "*Phantasticknesse*" as a "function / Even of the bright immortal part of man" (2.250). Later, in the most famous speech in

the play, Lampatho describes his lengthy study and the ultimate
futility of isolated book-learned theory. When he wonders what to do
in an age that spurns the scholar, Quadratus mockingly tells him to
cut his losses and "row with the tide." The varied fortunes of
Lampatho the would-be lover are no more realistic girds at Jonson
than was Phylomuse's turnabout in the face of Doricus's arguments in
the Induction. They represent the behavior of a Lampatho who is
only incidentally suggestive of Jonson the man in real life: whether
Jonson understood them as reflecting upon his own private behavior
is a question which cannot be answered. Nor need it be, for
Lampatho serves Marston's end well enough in the framework of the
quarrel as a vehicle to scorn the sort of gloomy, insincere malcontentedness by which he thought Jonson tainted and as a figure who
mocked, incidentally, certain well-known traits in Jonson's personality.

Jonson makes no reference to *What you Will* in *Poetaster*, but such
is the all-embracing ridicule poured on Marston in the play that a
particular reply was not needed. Jonson was fully roused; he had
endured the "laxative tongues" of his taunters for nearly three years
by the time *Poetaster* was ready. Envy begins the play with some
harsh words about players that the recipients were not soon to let
Jonson forget. Then an armed Prologue appears, armed because of
the dangerous days "Wherein, who writes, had neede present his
Scenes/Fortie-fold proofe against the conjuring meanes/Of base
detractors, and illiterate apes" (Pro. 7–9). The play leaves no one in
any doubt that first amongst such apes, "that common spawne of
ignorance / Our frie of writers" (18–19), is Marston, Rufus Laberius
Crispinus, a "ranke, and tedious foule," ceaseless talker full of "lewd
soloecismes, and worded trash." His physical traits are mentioned,
idiosyncrasies such as his snobbery are noted, but his poetic
pretensions receive the full weight of the attack. Marston's style in its
most extravagant vein is not hard to satirize, but Jonson does a
wickedly good job:

> Rampe up, my *genius;* be not retrograde;
> But boldly nominate a spade, a spade.
> What, shall thy lubricall and glibberie *Muse*
> Live, as shee were defunct, like punke in stewes?
> Alas! That were no moderne consequence,
> To have cothurnall buskins frighted hence.
> No; teach thy *incubus* to poetize;
> And throw abroad thy spurious snotteries,

> Upon that puft-up lumpe of barmy froth,
> Or clumsie chil-blain'd judgement.

(5.3.275–84)

The target is unmistakable, and the hits are palpable. Upon this specimen, Crispinus-Marston is judged and found guilty of being one of those who will

> gnaw their absent friends, not cure their fame,
> Catch at the loosest laughters, and affect
> To be thought jesters, such, as can devise
> Things never seene, or heard, t'impaire mens names,
> And gratifie their credulous adversaries,
> Will carrie tales, doe basest offices.

(5.3.329–35)

Horace-Jonson is acquitted on every charge laid against him by Crispinus and company and is revealed as "suffering vertue . . . The honest Satyre." Some of Horace's pills are administered to Crispinus, and he shortly begins to groan and vomit up the worst monstrosities of his vocabulary, including "glibbery," "lubricall," "spurious snot-teries," "chilblain'd," "clumsie," "barmy froth," "puffy," "turgid-ous," "ventositous," "oblatrant," "furibund," "fatuate," "strenuous" (almost the first thing Crispinus said was that he was "most strenuously well") and "quaking custard" (a phrase he must many times have regretted ever using).

After this regurgitation there is hope, but not certainty, of cure and so a rigorous diet of the best Classical authors is prescribed and he is warned: "You must not hunt for wild, out-landish termes, / To stuffe out a peculiar *dialect:* / But let your *matter* runne before your *words*" (5.3.549–57). As a criticism of style, Jonson's words were just, and it is to Marston's credit that he took them to heart. *The Malcontent,* his next play, was less extravagant in language and possibly the published text, in 1607, of *What You Will* also benefited from judicious pruning, perhaps of some of those vomited words not found in any of his extant work.

However, the immediate question was not the justness of Jonson's criticisms but how best to answer them. Dekker, presumably with Marston's ready assistance, quickly wrote a good-humored and sprightly reply to Jonson. Then, happily unhampered by any Jonsonian ideas of dramatic propriety, he thrust it with splendid nonchalance into an otherwise undistinguished romantic historical play he was working on and called the whole thing, *Satiromastix:* both the answer and its framework were calculated to irritate Jonson.

Rough and effective as was Jonson's handling of Marston, *Poetaster* had won him no popular approval. Imbued with that serene confidence in his own righteousness and in his grand stature as a poet, Jonson was his own worst enemy and alienated his hearers. Thus, besides applying his whips and scorns to Marston and Dekker, which would not in itself have greatly disturbed many people, he managed to offend playwrights and players at the public theaters as a body. The last word, therefore, in all ways, was with Jonson's opponents. He was left to reflect upon what he had never doubted, that he was the better poet and playwright and that his was the better play, all of which probably soothed him little when it was so clear that *Satiromastix* was more popular, funnier, and, despite the fact that it did not spare Jonson, better natured than *Poetaster. Satiromastix* was more comic in tone: Jonson makes a better comic butt than does Marston. Jonson's charges of plagiarism against Dekker and Marston are not proven, but their accusations about his arrogance, self-love, and railing tone are. In brief, "The Poetasters-in-chief have made out the better case."[5]

The surprising upshot was that both Jonson and Marston retired from the turmoil and became, at least for some months, friends. Jonson turned to tragedy. Marston, who was silent for two years, then produced *The Malcontent,* which was certainly the best play he had yet written, but which was also dedicated to Jonson, as his sincere and wise friend. A year later, Marston, Chapman, and Jonson collaborated in producing one of the best London comedies, *Eastward Hoe.*

CHAPTER 5

Satiric Poet into Satiric Dramatist

I Verse Satire and the Stage

WHEN Marston began writing plays, he took into the theater the themes and the material of his satires. The similarities between the modes of verse satire and satiric drama were deceptive, and the extent of the gap between the two was one of the first things Marston discovered. His strength in satire had been in content, not in form; his abundant satiric imagination, delight in detail, willingness to digress, and his fervor in debate demanded a control which he never found easy to institute. As a result, his verse lacked strong formal organization. The reader was carried through it, albeit somewhat bruised and dazed, primarily by the reiteration of a point of view and by the emotional force of the argument.

In the theater, however, there has to be a narrative structure. Figures in the satires exist as demonstrations of an idea; and, since they come before the reader as illustrations of an argument, he is indifferent to their life histories. When they quit the printed page for the stage, the situation changes, for, unlike the reader, the spectator wants to know who the character before him is, where he comes from, where he is going, why he speaks and behaves as he does, and what his relationship is to others in the play. In the verse satire, characteristics were enough; in the play, characters are demanded. The satiric poet, that is, can do without a narrative, but the satiric dramatist cannot.

In the general sense of the word, verse satires were "dramatic," insofar as they were vivid, spirited, and full of emotion. They came yet closer to the drama in their use of lively situations, their presentation of sharply etched human traits of behavior, and, above all, in their colloquiality. Marston's satires are especially rich in voices; he exploits his own keen ear for speech differences by letting

55

his victims give themselves away by some apt turn of phrase or trick of speech. These are all excellent ingredients for drama, but the satires are nonetheless not a series of dramatic sketches that only need to be strung together on the stage to make a play. The vigor of its statements cannot disguise the fact that satire is essentially a static art, whereas drama is a dynamic one.

To rely on inherent dramatic qualities of the satires (as to a certain extent Marston did in the main part of *Histriomastix*) and to transfer them to the stage directly with commentary by a relatively detached figure does not make a play. The result is a dramatic recitation of satires which is not the same thing as a satiric drama. Not surprisingly, therefore, none of the conventional modes of drama gave satisfying accomodation to Marston's ideas. His realization of this fact is reflected in the fun he made of them. When Phylomuse is asked in the Induction to *What You Will*, "Ist Commedy, Tragedy, Pastorall, Morall, Nocturnal or Historie?" he replies: "Faith perfectly neither, but even *What You Will*" (Ind. 2.233). Something more bluntly to the same purpose is the list of plays offered in *Histriomastix* for performance by Sir Oliver Owlet's men:

> *Mother Gurtons needle;* (a Tragedy.)
> *The Divell and Dives;* (a Comedie.)
> *A russet coate, and a Knaves cap;* (an Infernall.)
> *A proud heart and a beggars purse;* (a pastorall.)
> *The Widdowes apron-strings;* (a nocturnall.)
>
> (3.263)

In accord with these mysterious descriptions, the play they perform begins as the romance of Troilus and Cressida and changes boldly and inconsequentially into a very old-fashioned morality play. Marston might have found a similar difficulty in categorizing his own plays, for each of his first five plays represents a different approach to the problem of finding the most satisfying mold for his ideas.

At various times, both in earnest and in burlesque, and not necessarily in one play at a time, Marston essays "Commedy, Tragedy, Pastorall, Morall, Nocturnal or Historie." The titles of his plays suggest his quizzical attitude toward definition. *Histriomastix or The Player Whipt* marks an emphasis on satire but gives no indication that it is, in fact, a morality play. *Jacke Drum's Entertainment* is precisely that—an entertaining grab bag of assorted situations and events. By subtitle, it is *The Comedie of Pasquill and Katherine*, but their hazardous love affair uneasily combines "The Perils of Pauline" and Shakespeare's *Romeo and Juliet*. If it is a "comedie," it is of an odd kind. The two parts of *The Historie of Antonio and Mellida* explore romantic melodrama, satirical comedy, and bloody revenge tragedy in accord with Marston's assertion that he wrote them in a vein deliberately a little "humorous" and "seriously fantasticall" (1.2). *What You Will* pithily defies pigeonholing.

II   Histriomastix or The Player Whipt

Histriomastix is a rather old-fashioned allegory in the morality play vein that is mostly moderate in tone and is, therefore, rather an odd work to follow on the heels of *The Scourge of Villanie*. The play, which is divided into six acts, depicts the movement from a state of Peace through Plenty, Pride, Envy, War, and Poverty to a return to Peace. Each act (except Envy's) is introduced by the grand entry of its central allegorical figure and her adherents and supporters. After introductory speeches by them, the behavior of different persons from various walks of life is noticed—of common people, merchants, lawyers, young noblemen, strolling players, and the general commentator, Chrisoganus. This conspectus of society and its behavior under certain conditions provides a theme not very different from that of the verse satires. The immediate difference is that the cycle of progress provides Marston with a framework that imposes an order upon his commentaries. This order, however, is not a plot; and much of *Histriomastix* reads like a recitation of a verse satire rather than a play. Characters appear on the stage only as mouthpieces for Marston's opinions; they stand and talk but give no other sign of life. In act 4, for instance, the speech headings could be shuffled about with no loss or gain to the revelations of the working of Envy. During the course of the play, the characters merely react to whatever is the state of affairs; they do not change. Chrisoganus rises above their dilemma by disdaining the false shows of the world with a stoic calm, and, at the end of the play, his lessons are generously welcomed by society, but only with the same characterless necessity that had ruled their earlier reactions to situations in the play.

This inability to infuse the representations of modes of behavior and belief with dramatic life is emphasized by the liveliness with which the strolling players, Sir Oliver Owlet's men, are treated. They benefit from having a simple story to tell, rather than having to serve only as examples of reaction to certain conditions; those about them

react, but these men have something to act out. The troupe also
presents an audacious and amusing mockery of the adult companies
in the public theaters. Owlet's men are tradesmen fallen upon hard
times. Because they can already manage singing, and a little mimicry,
they reckon that a smattering of practice will enable them to put on
plays.

Their playwright is Post-hast, a poor scribbling hack with a thin
pride at being a poet rather than merely a player: he is recognizably
meant for Anthony Munday, a vigorous anti-Catholic pamphleteer
and middling but persistent playwright. The troupe's work is all
marked by blundering ineptitude. Not surprisingly the sample of
their talents presented before the Lord Mavortius is "base-browne-
paper-stuffe," which begins as a romance of Troilus and Cressida and
abruptly concludes as concentrated morality: "Enter a roaring *Divell*
with the *Vice* on his back, *Iniquity* in one hand; and *Juventus* in the
other" (3.265). Their alcoholic muse does not long sustain them, the
onset of war ruins their fortunes, and they are rounded up for
vagabonds and transported overseas.

Marston tells the story of Owlet's men in something of the same
manner that they gave their own play—theirs is a hurried presentation of snatches and sketches of scenes and situations with none fully
worked out. Marston hustles these characters on stage, lets them
suggest a scene, and then hustles them off again. Nonetheless, their
slender activity is the only life of which *Histriomastix* can boast; for,
apart from Chrisoganus, theirs are the only voices tinged with
individuality.

The most surprising thing about the play is its moderation of tone.
Only Chrisoganus occasionally vents opinions in Marston's spluttering invective style. The influence of the bishops' order of 1599 may be
one reason for this restraint, but there are others. It has been argued
that, for his first venture on the stage, Marston chose to adapt an old
morality play, altering little in the first two acts, but largely rewriting
the remainder. This would explain the general structure of the play,
the un-Marstonian passages found in it, and the odd melange which
Owlet's men present. However, it would not be very odd that
Marston should have consciously chosen to model his first play on
morality lines. As for the language, the verse satires show that he did
not habitually write in an angrily aggressive manner and that he was
quite capable of writing all the parts of *Histriomastix*. The ineptitude
of the little show produced by Owlet's men is an apt example of their
productions and, by inference, those of the public theaters, crude as

the parody may be, rather than proof of Marston's revising hand. Although he may have been revising an old play, it is equally possible that he wrote it himself.

That *Histriomastix* was performed is known from a reference in Jonson's *Every Man Out Of His Humour* in 1599, but where is not known. Doubts and problems are largely resolved by Philip Finkelpearl's suggestion that Marston wrote the play for the Middle Temple Christmas festivities of 1598–99. This resolution would introduce Marston as a dramatist prior to the revival of the boys' companies toward the end of 1599 when the Children of Paul's, for whom Marston became a leading playwright, began acting. Finkelpearl's view also adds force to Marston's father's references to "playes vayne studdyes and fooleryes" in his will. It would also partly explain the rather stiff, tableau-like structure of the piece and the luxurious calls on the number of actors which it makes (there are at least 153 name parts; however, with slight cutting and much doubling, the whole thing could have been managed with a company of 20 and would not have been beyond the powers of a boys' company).

If *Histriomastix* is accepted as a "traditional celebration of law and order in which Marston emphasized the contribution of the liberal arts and its learned masters to the health of the commonwealth" (hence the dismissal of Owlet, Post-hast, and their disorderly troupe), part of that tradition demanded a play "designed to afford opportunities for declamation by as many young gentlemen as possible".[1] In this case, what is a criticism of it as a regular stage play—the ineffective arrangement of its material, its being really a series of scenes illustrative of themes and ideas—becomes a recognition of its virtues, or at least acceptability, as an entertainment for the Middle Temple society.

Nonetheless, the matter and the style of *Histriomastix* indicate several things about Marston's natural talents for the stage. These capabilities are rough and undisciplined, but they appear within the traditional didactic entertainment because a stage play keeps struggling to emerge. The plot of the rise and fall of the strolling players is developed in the spasmodic, hasty manner to mark much of Marston's method of handling a plot. As for characterization, he treats that as cavalierly as he did rhyme; he was not yet able to adjust the meaning of the character to the development of the individual speaker. For example, Chrisoganus emerges as an individual, but his transformation from fussy pedant to railing critic is roughly managed, and his effectiveness is blunted by the puppets who surround him.

The players and the common people in the market sound like real people; but, as soon as one of them begins to talk at length, his vividness is replaced by the characterless tone of the lecturer.

Marston's language is not always dull and ineffective, even though it lacks the variety of individual voices. The best verse is found in some of Chrisoganus's speeches and in the introductory sections to the acts. This verse is packed and incisive: it is sometimes overfull of ideas, it is sometimes clogged by images that reach too boldly after their effect, but it is dramatic and effective. The description of the ravages of war in the fifth act is a good example of this better verse, and the injunction to war itself is typical of both the firm and the faltering qualities found in the verse:

> Meane while weele steepe our sinowie feet in blood
> And daunce unto the Musicke of the field,
> Trumpets for trebbles, bases, bellowing drummes.
> Broyles Envy bred, but Warre shall end those brawles,
> Deafe warre that will not heare a word of Peace:
> Sharpe pikes shall serve for subtle lawiers pens
> The Marchants silkes shall turne to shining steele,
> In steed of false-yard stickes, large horsemens staves,
> Shall measure out true pattern's of their graves.
>
> (3.285)

Since Marston always had had a tendency to be theatrical rather than dramatic in his writing, the stage provided him with a fitter outlet for this flamboyant side of his personality than had his verse satires. From the first, he had displayed an eager interest in theatrical effects; and the generally uninteresting flow of *Histriomastix* is, from time to time, startlingly interrupted by some bold or surprising theatrical effect. His willingness to experiment and his anxiety that his effects should be properly staged is shown in this drama, as in all his plays, by careful stage directions. Steady maintenance of action in the broadest sense was never his strongest suit, but he could always create incidental moments of activity. The riots of the fifth act, for instance, are carefully controlled, and the text contains these three directions:

Enter a sort of fellowes with armour and weapons and crosse the stage crying arme, arme, arme.

Enter a *Captaine* with *Souldiers:* the *Souldiers* having most of the *Players* apparrell; and bringing out the *Players* among'st them.

. . . .

Enter all the factions of *Noblemen, Peasants,* and *Cittizens* fighting: the ruder sorte drive in the rest and cry a sacke, a sacke, Havoke havocke, Burne the Lawiers bookes; teare the Silkes out of the shops: in that confusion: the *Scholler* scaping from among them, they all go out and leave him upon the Stage.

(3.291)

The tableaux which open each act are quite carefully arranged so that they would not be unduly repetitive and be differentiated only in the person of their leading figure. All in all, *Histriomastix*, which gave Marston the security of a theme very like that dealt with in his satires with the additional benefit of a framework, provided practice in stagecraft and, if nothing else, revealed to him the problems of plotting and characterization.

III Jacke Drum's Entertainment or the Comedie of Pasquill and Katherine

Although satire interrupted by bursts of action is the mark of *Histriomastix, Jacke Drum's Entertainment* is a cheerful medley of entertainments packed with action and a cast of clearly differentiated but somewhat oversimplified characters. Since the mood of the play is not congenial to satire, burlesque and lighthearted parody replace it. Marston tries to give shape to this variety by lavish plotwork, but he was to discover that even richly plotted plays still need a dramatist's controlling hand.

In this drama, the jovial Sir Edward Fortune has two marriageable daughters, Katherine and Camelia. They may choose whom they will for a husband, for their father's only stipulation is that, rich or poor, he must be a gentleman. Katherine loves Pasquil and rejects the usurer, Mamon. In revenge, Mamon hires the Frenchman, Monsieur John fo de King, to kill Pasquil. Monsieur merely adds to his money by revealing this plan to the intended victim who pretends to be dead in order to terrify Mamon. Katherine, who is not aware of this plan, becomes so deranged when she hears that Pasquil is dead that she becomes suicidal; but such a death is prevented by the reappearance of Pasquil. This relief is temporary; for, while Pasquil leaves to fetch her cloak (she had appeared clad only in her petticoat),

Mamon returns, throws poison in her face, and so disfigures her that she flees. Her disappearance causes Pasquil to go mad. Meanwhile, Katherine has found treatment for her scars at the hands of a herbal woman and recovers her old beauty. Pasquil is cured by the aid of quiet music and by the return of his Katherine, and they finally retire to happiness ever after.

Katherine's sister, Camelia, a stupid, flighty creature, loves any man her maid Winifred praises; and the maid's praises are for sale and are bought by Ellis with the result that Brabant, Jr., who loves Camelia, is ignored by her. Infuriated by this rejection, Brabant, Jr.'s friend, Planet, outbids Ellis so that he may scornfully reject Camelia when she comes to him. Because Planet has neglected to tell his friend about his plan, Brabant, Jr., angry at what he thinks is a betrayal, arranges for Planet's death and is narrowly prevented from committing suicide himself. Needless to say, deaths are avoided; complexities are made clear; and Camelia is justly punished as, at the end of the play, she turns futilely from one man to another.

This précis is but the outline of the complicated, death-shadowed love affairs of the daughters, for there is also Winifred's own gulling of her two lovers and Brabant, Sr.'s self-cuckoldry. With characteristic fervor, Marston has gone to the other extreme from the formality of *Histriomastix* and has written an overplotted play crammed with incident. In similar fashion, a large selection of characters is crowded into this play, but, although one or two show signs of bursting the bonds of conventionality, such signs are only briefly seen. For example, Sir Edward begins as an interesting individual, but he quickly sinks into the stereotyped jovial squire. Katherine is the simple heroine who is matched in her ardors, in her suicidal tendencies, and in her madness by Pasquil. Winifred is the pert maid; Mamon is the incredibly evil usurer; and Brabant, Sr., Puffe, Monsieur, and Ellis are stock types of the braggart, fop, foreigner, and foolish gentleman, respectively. One or two persons fill several roles, but there is no complication as they move swiftly from one to the other. For example, Brabant, Jr. is by turn the straight man to Planet, the romantic lover, and the young man fallen to evil ways; Planet is the critic and commentator who takes a closer hand in affairs than his predecessor Chrisoganus did in his play.

Because of such contrivances, Marston had seemingly decided to use as many of the stock characters and theatrical devices as he could. In fact, he impudently uses himself as the first stock character to appear on stage in his new play. The tyer-man opens the play with a hasty apology for a fracas behind the scenes because the author "hath snatched" the script from the players "and with violence keepes the boyes from comming on the Stage" (3.179). As usual, Marston has been misunderstood by his critic! He was merely concerned that neither his play nor his actors were good enough, explains one of the boy actors. The seemingly uneasy author-actor is, however, quite certain of the superiority of his wares to those too often offered; for he promises the audience that his "pleasing sceanes" will be fresh and will have nothing to do "With mouldy fopperies of stale Poetry,/ Unpossible drie mustie Fictions" (3.179).

Marston, in fact, is merrily guying the staid citizen comedies and the romantic histories of star-crossed lovers. His intention in his play is clear enough, but the action is so seriously undertaken at moments that the general mood of lighthearted jollity does not quite disguise the serious implications. The whole action of Planet's device to teach Camelia a lesson and its effect on Brabant, Jr. does not ring with exactly the cheerful note of the rest of the play. Elsewhere, the old problem of trying to decide whether a scene or situation is a parody or a poor attempt at the real thing mars the overall impression; for example, Katherine is prepared to kill herself because she thinks that Pasquil is dead (3.214–15). Yet behind these passing doubts lies the possibility that the whole play with its throbbing actions, its array of thwarted deaths, and its melodramatic twists and turns is a parody. To write such a wholehearted parody demands a steadiness of aim and a refusal to attempt a scene or situation for its own sake rather than for the purpose of making fun of it. Whatever the essential purpose of the play, it is hampered by a lack of unity; the comical atmosphere fails to hold the material together.

That Marston could introduce more serious matters without letting them disturb the balance is proved by his treatment of love and marriage in the play. In the first act, Sir Edward speaks sensibly and convincingly on this topic, and, when he becomes merely the convivial host, his views are adopted by Planet. In the beginning, Sir Edward's philosophy of life represents the sane counterpart to that practiced by the endless procession of vice-ridden men whom Marston had also attacked in his verse satires. Sir Edward sees the folly of the times and would rather hear the morris dancers talk sensibly of the small things they know about than pretentious young men about matters of which they are ignorant. Mamon's miserly way with money is decried: "I had rather live rich to die poore, then live poore to die rich," declares Sir Edward (3.184):

I long not to be squeasd with mine owne waight:
Nor hoyse up all my sailes to catch the winde
Of the drunke reeling Commons: I labor not
To have an awfull presence, nor be feard.
. . . .
And after death like Chesmen having stood
In play for Bishops, some for Knights, and Pawnes,
We all together shall be tumbled up, into one bagge,
Let hush'd calme quiet, rock my life a sleepe.

                                                                    (3.184–85)

Katherine's refusal of Mamon is upheld by Sir Edward:

Nay be free my daughters in election,
. . . . . but o when time shall search
The strength of love, then vertue, and your eye,
Must knit his sinewes: I chusde my selfe a wife
Poore, but of good dissent, and we did live
Till death divorc'd us, as a man would wish:
I made a woman, now wenches make a man;
Chuse one either of valour, wit, honestie, or wealth,
So he be gentle, and you have my heart,
Ifaith you have.

                                                                    (3.186–87)

The hectic onrush of the action leaves no room for the unusual and
appealing character of Sir Edward, and the genuine feeling about
love and marriage which he expresses is lost in the frivolity and
melodrama. It reappears fleetingly in Brabant, Jr's serious plea to
Camelia to accept him, younger brother and poor man though he be:

Coach Jades and Dogges, are coupled still together,
Only for outward likenes, growth and strength,
But the bright models of eternitie,
Are joind together for affection,
Which in the soule is form'de. Oh let this move,
Love should make mariage, and not mariage Love.

                                                                    (3.212)

Planet advises him to forget Camelia and inveighs against the
mercenary marriages of the times. After Brabant, Jr. leaves, he
arranges for Winifred to bribe Camelia to his love and plans her

downfall. The nature of the trick and the reasons for it lead him to express, more bitterly than Sir Edward, views about women that are reminiscent of Marston's satires. As Planet's denunciations are terser and less extravagant, Marston is able, though them, to make his points about love and lust with more reason and more effectiveness than before. Camelia pleads with Planet, and he rebuffs her:

> o that the soules of men
> Were temperate like mine, then Natures painte
> Should not triumph o're our infirmities.
> I do adore with infinit respect,
> Weomen whose merit issues from their worth
> Of inward graces, but these rotten poasts
> That are but guilt with outward garnishment,
> O how my soule abhorres them.
>
> (3.229)

Here, for once, Marston treats temperately the theme of true and feigned love and the rottenness of many women which so often had led him into excess in his verse satires.

The hints of development shown here and elsewhere in the play, he later worked out fully and deeply in *The Dutch Curtezan*, but he sacrifices such development in *Jacke Drum's Entertainment* because of the demands of farce and of melodrama. Brabant, Jr., Planet, and Sir Edward voice some of his firmest convictions; but there are other jobs for them to do, and they are brusquely called from dramatic to theatrical business. As has been noted, it is particularly sad that Marston was unable to sustain his characterization of Sir Edward as the jovial father whose heartiness expressed genuine and sympathetic views of living. Ironically, Sir Edward's interest as a character is scuttled by his being a rich, jovial man. Convention beats down the individual life in him; for just as his casual mention of morris dancers has not been let pass without having a group of dancers roister on and perform, so the opportunity he gives for conventional jollity as a bibulous squire cannot be ignored by a Marston eager to demonstrate his versatility and ability to provide theatrical entertainment. Sir Edward soon calls, therefore, for sack to carouse away the loss of his daughter Katherine. Such incidents make it seem that Marston's interest in sustaining the character flagged and was jostled aside by his eagerness to try other sorts of scenes and situations.

Some of these scenes are excellently contrived and well managed.

The sequence of serenades to Katherine which opens the second act is cleverly used. Puffe, a lesser Cloten, offers one which is a faithful reproduction of his own vaporings. As he departs, Mamon, who testily enters, is saving an inch of candle because daylight is appearing. He sings of his money more than of Katherine, and the "chuncks" sound typically and ironically through his song. When Pasquil enters, Marston does not fall into the trap of a third song but displays him as a Romeo. The parodic love songs are followed by the desperate rhetoric of an inept Romeo that reminds us of Inamorato Curio (SV, 8), as well as the farewells of Hermia and Lysander in *A Midsummer Nights Dream:*

PAS: The heavens shall melt, the sun shall cease to shine,
           Before I leave the love of *Katherine*
KATH: Nay when heavens melted, & the sun strooke dead,
           Even then my love shall not be vanquished.
PAS: When I turne fickle, vertue shall be vice.
KATH: When I prove false, Hell shall be Paradice.
PAS: My life shall be maintaind by thy kind breath.
KATH: Thy love shall be my life, thy hate my death.

                                        (3.199)

This crisp volley of exchanges ends with Katherine replying with her own version of Juliet's lingering farewell (the concision may help in lending an air of parody to it):

          But now no more, bright day malings our love,
          Farewell, yet stay, but tis no matter too,
          My Father knowes I thinke, what must ensue.
          Adieu, yet harke, nay faith, adieu, adiew.

                                        (3.200)

The action following this exchange is in Marston's most shorthand manner, for high-flown rhetoric decorates some indefatigably melo-dramatic events. The suspicion that he may have intended some sharper impact from these events than one is ready to allow remains, but their furious succession, their excess, and their brevity strongly suggest tongue-in-cheek. The mark of the play is grotesque humor and farce; but the battery of devices he uses suggests a writer who is trying his hand at everything and who, at times, is so carried away by what he is mocking that he abjures the mockery.

IV   Antonio and Mellida

The Historie of Antonio and Mellida displays all Marston's most characteristic qualities, good and bad, not the least of which is his managing, as Una Ellis-Fermor has noted, to "contrive the effects in his plays so as to leave in our minds a vivid impression of something close to the dramatic."[2] An examination of some of the contrivances in *The Historie* enables one to define more narrowly that closeness to the dramatic. As for Marston's plot, the troubles borne by lovers sprung from the fatal loins of families bitterly divided by ancient grudges supplied the ground for many Elizabethan plays. In *The Historie*, Andrugio, Duke of Genoa, defeated at sea by Piero Sforza, Duke of Venice, finds refuge in the marshes near Venice; and his son Antonio also escapes after the sea battle. He and Mellida, daughter of Piero, are in love; and, disguised as an Amazon, he goes to Piero's court. When the lovers decide to flee to England, Piero almost frustrates their plan; but they manage to reach the marshes outside Venice. Mellida is quickly recaptured, however, and is returned to court and to a planned dynastic marriage.

Antonio is in despair; and Andrugio, now reunited with his son, takes matters into his own hands. Disdaining any longer to live in hiding, he goes to Piero's court where, asserting that he has brought the head of the hunted Andrugio, he removes his helm and demands death. Piero, overcome by this gesture, forswears vengeance and promises his enduring honor to and love for Andrugio. When a coffin is carried in containing Antonio's body, Piero amid renewed grief, asserts that he would give his life, and his daughter's hand, if only Antonio were alive. At this moment, Antonio rises from the coffin, Piero agrees to his betrothal to Mellida, and all ends with promises of happiness.

Few Elizabethan plots sound convincing in such a bald outline, but the playwright's strong imagination has created such tricks that he can amend the "unpossible drie mustie Fictions" into the motive and cues for passion. Marston finds dramatic conviction in the contrivances and extravagances of the situation even as he stresses their silliness and artificiality. Since he stresses the imbalances of his story, Antonio and Mellida are treated as figures not only of romance and passion, but also of satire and comedy. They remind one in turn of Romeo and Juliet, Troilus and Cressida, and Pyramus and Thisbe.

Marston does not ask a simple response to his story; he handles his story so ambiguously that it is sometimes difficult to assess how much ambiguity is due to Marston's careful planning and how much is an unwitting (or even candid) reflection of his own uncertainty in handling his material. But boldness is his friend, and it lends the play its vivacity and momentary urgency.

Marston ensures an ambiguity of response by prefacing his play with an Induction that stresses that what is to follow is essentially a performance—a playing of parts by uncommitted actors who clearly have no overall unifying conception of the play.

The Induction is set in the green room; the actors discuss the peculiar problems posed by their roles rather uncertainly, and method actors they certainly are not: "Faith, we can say our parts," admits the boy whose role is Piero Sforza, "but wee are ignorant in what mould we must cast our Actors." The leader of the troupe, who seems to play the roles of both Alberto and Andrugio, settles Piero's problem:

> O, ho: then thus frame your exterior shape,
> To hautie forme of elate majestie;
> As if you held the palsey shaking head
> Of reeling chaunce, under your fortunes belt
> In strictest vassalage: growe big in thought,
> As swolne with glory of successfull armes.
>
> (1.5)

The young Piero pertly replies, "Who can not be proud, stroak up the haire, and strut!"; and he acts out the boy's impression of a proud nobleman. Antonio, who sabotages the romantic hero by his petulance at having to disguise himself as a lady, complains in his boy's voice, "I a voice to play a lady! I shall nere doe it" (1.7). Alberto will hear none of this: "Not play two parts in one? away, away: 'tis common fashion. Nay if you cannot bear two subtle fronts under one hood, Ideot goe by, goe by; off this world's stage!" (1.7).

This exchange touches upon a common theme of the verse satires that is translated directly into theatrical terms: the hypocritical duplicity of a villainous society becomes the necessary pretense of the stage. Alberto is both drama coach and cynical commentator on manners. Next Matzagente demonstrates his powers in the Ercles vein: "By the bright honour of a *Millanoise*, and the resplendent fulgor of this steele, I will defende the feminine to death; and ding his spirit to the verge of hell, that dares divulge a Ladies' prejudice."

Feliche affects astonishment as he deflates this windy rhetoric: "Rampum scrampum, mount tuftie *Tamburlaine*. What rattling thunderclappe breakes from his lips?" (1.7). Feliche then talks about his own role: his name means "the contented man"; and, as the appointed commentator upon the superficiality of court life, he has an important role in defining the tone and mode of the play. He is the persona of the verse satires translated into dramatic terms.

Feliche's role is to be one who is "steddie, and must seeme so impregnably fortrest with his own content, that no envious thought could ever invade his spirit . . as farre from envying any man, as he valued all men infinitely distant from accomplisht beatitude" (1.8). In act 1, he is such a man, and he rebukes Piero's arrogance with quiet firmness. Later, he analyzes the quality of his own settled calm only to be driven within minutes to rage by the behavior of the foppish courtiers. The calm observer and the railing malcontent are in conflict within him; and, although he is a good ringmaster to the court circus and avoids the harsher extremes that Marston could too easily reach, his plain man outburst breaks the satiric balance, the mood of the stage world.

V *Conflict and Contradiction in Character*

The first-night audience would have found the Induction, for all its amusing liveliness, a puzzling guide to a puzzling play. The actors' querying of the range of action asked of their characters proves to be well founded, for "The hautie forme of elate majestie" expected of Piero does not foretell his spluttering reaction to the news that Mellida plans to defy his authority:

Run, keepe the Palace, post to the ports, goe to my daughters chamber: whether now? scud to the Jewes, stay, runne to the gates, stop the gundolets, let none passe the marsh, doe all at once. *Antonio?* his head, his head. Keep you the Court, the rest stand still, or runne, or goe, or shoute, or search, or scud, or call, or hang, or doe doe doe, su su su, somthing: I know not who who who, what I do do do, nor who who who, where I am.   (1.39)

This naturalistic outburst is both frightening and funny; but, if he rages like Herod, he does not kill like him. The effect produced is characteristic: it follows a leisurely scene of courtiers who are primping before mirrors, it violently replaces that picture of an idle court with one of an urgent and potentially savage court, and then it

lets the danger collapse in its own splutter. In the last act, Piero is the
burly, jovial ruler; and his instant acceptance of Andrugio's nobility is
unexpected but conventional and sincere. In *Antonio's Revenge*,
Piero claims that this attitude toward Antonio was masterly dissimulation; but his assertion is only the view from part 2 and has no
relevance to part 1.

Andrugio can decline to coarse patriotic anger, but he generally
commands attention by his noble endurance and by his fine
expression of it. The mockery of the Induction cannot hold against
these reflections:

> Why man, I never was a Prince till now.
> Tis not the bared pate, the bended knees,
> Guilt tipstaves, Tyrrian purple, chaires of state,
> Troopes of pide butterflies, that flutter still
> In greatnesse summer, that confirme a prince:
> Tis not the unsavory breath of multitudes,
> Showting and clapping, with confused dinne;
> That makes a Prince. No, *Lucio,* he's a king,
> A true right king, that dares doe aught, save wrong,
> Feares nothing mortall, but to be unjust,
> Who is not blowne up with the flattering puffes
> Of spungy Sycophants: Who stands unmov'd,
> Despight the justling of opinion:
>
> (1.44)

Romantic heroes were never Marston's strength, and Antonio is
undermined by clever, rather than convincing, experiments. After
being exposed by the Induction, he has to begin the play proper in his
disdained Amazon disguise. His opening soliloquy is sufficiently
vigorous to overcome memories of the actor's unease at the disguise,
only for it to end with a direct reference to his being in disguise. The
old device for the heroine's masquerading as a boy is reversed to no
purpose, for the hero disguised as a young girl only loses authority. At
moments of stress, Antonio tends to faint and grovel helplessly; and
this action may pass the first time it is performed because of his
feminine disguise; but, on repetition, it is decidedly feeble. In
addition, the accumulation of self-pitying speeches allows Antonio
hardly any masculine assertiveness. If the unfortunate comparisons
between what is ordinarily expected of the romantic hero and what
Antonio actually does are intentional on Marston's part, then they are

conceived as parody; but parody and sincerity stand awkwardly side by side.

Marston's characters are not only at odds with their society, but often with themselves. Antonio discusses in the Induction his role with Feliche and harps on this point:

> Now as solemne as a travailer, and as grave as a Puritanes ruffe: with the same breath as slight and scatterd in his fashion as—as—as a—a — any thing. Now, as sweet and neat as a Barbours casting-bottle; straight as slovenly as the yeasty breast of an Ale-knight: now, lamenting: then chafing: straight laughing: then—
> FEL: What then?
> ANT: Faith I know not what: 'tad bene a right part for *Proteus* or *Gew:* ho, blinde *Gew* would ha don't rarely, rarely.   (1.8).

Andrugio's expressions of noble fortitude contrast so sharply with the rotten society around him that attention is drawn to the forced comparison as much as to any implied moral. Such a mood is set in the satirical and gaily comical scenes that it is perhaps a question whether the characters can claim immunity to farce when it is required, and whether their serious words can sustain themselves amid the general comic noise.

Marston's attitude toward his story dictates how his characters will appear. The plot interests him only insofar as it provides opportunity for exercises in the emotions—pride, fortitude, despair, melancholy, ardor, pathos, anger, bitterness—but these exercises are rhetorical rather than dramatic, and more attention is paid to acting out passions than to acting out the story. Marston is more concerned, therefore, with peoples' reactions to a situation than with the situation itself. As a result, the narrative moves hectically, but sporadically. The story is illustrated rather than told, and the excitement resides in the variety and force of the illustrations and the contrasts they make with one another.

The strength and weakness of Marston's method is illustrated in the fourth act. When Antonio enters, distraught at having lost touch with Mellida in their flight from Piero's court, he begins to expostulate feebly; but the verse then miraculously achieves perfectly the blended strength and precision that struggle to emerge from a good deal of Marston's verse:

> Conceipt you me. As having clasp't a rose
> Within my palme, the rose being tane away,

My hand retaines a little breath of sweete:
So may man's trunke; his spirit slipt awaie,
Hold still a faint perfume of his sweet ghest.

(1.43)

This level, which is maintained as Antonio's submission to his grief, is naturalistically shown in the breakdown of his speech. While he sleeps, Andrugio enters; and Antonio's finely expressed but adolescent sentiments give place to his mature father's thoughts: "Why man, I never was a Prince till now." Reminded of his political and familial losses, he falls from these philosophic heights; and the long steady tread of the previous speeches gives way to an exchange of startled questions between father and son which builds to a tearfully pathetic reunion. When Andrugio goes to prepare a place for his son, Antonio, left alone, consoles himself with a song which he asks his page to sing. For once the extravagant Crispinine manner, to which Antonio now comes, is fitting, as its verbosity is perceptively treated as part of Antonio's self-appraisal. Indeed, Antonio manages perfectly that controlled wry comment on his overfluent manner which Marston sought so roughly in *Pigmalion's Image:*

Sing but, *Antonio* hath lost *Mellida,*
And thou shalt see mee (like a man possest)
Howle out such passion, that even this brinish marsh
Will squease out teares, from out his spungy cheekes,
The rocks even groane, and—
Pree thee, pree thee sing:
Or I shall nere ha done when I am in,
Tis harder for me end, then to begin.
    (The boy runnes a note, *Antonio* breakes it.)
For looke thee boy, my griefe that hath no end,
I may begin to playne, but—pree thee sing.

(1.47)

Mellida enters disguised as a page. With sad inevitability Antonio falls to the ground before playing Orlando to Mellida's Ganymede. Mellida finally doffs her disguise, and at this climactic moment the dialogue moves into Italian for eighteen lines. The effect is like an aria after recitative in opera, the lovers' ecstasy being marked by this switch of language. The "aria" moves matters onto another plane and clearly separates the reunion from what has gone before; but, in a play written in English, it is not a courageous, nor a sensible, experiment. The deflating remarks of Antonio's page also isolate this exchange: "I thinke confusion of *Babell* is falne upon these lovers, that they change their language; but I feare mee, my master having but fained the person of a woman, hath got their unfained imperfection, and is growne double tongu'd" (1.49). His presence during the meeting and his visible reactions before he speaks undoubtedly add to the curious effect of the scene.

Antonio and Mellida pursue their love in a world that has little time for them; the sardonic attitude of the page, the stoicism of Andrugio, and the relationship between him and his son push the love affair to one side. It could be poignant, but Marston's handling also tends to alienate the lovers from the audience. He attached great value to domestic love, but he associated overtly romantic ardor with lust and falsity: he shied from portraying it straightforwardly; and it may have been this desire to avoid that trap that drove him to try Italian.

The necessary capture of Mellida is arranged with a brutal lack of fuss. Antonio is sent to scout for pursuers so that they may enter as soon as he is gone. Although hardly the time for it, Balurdo provides excellent comedy as he tells how he mistook a cow for Mellida. As the most incompetent of the pursuers, it is ironic that he should discover Mellida. After the use made of the traditional impenetrability of stage disguises, this discovery neatly exposes their actual thinness. Mellida is hurried away; Antonio returns with Andrugio and is overwhelmed by the turn of events. He abjectly departs, leaving the stage to his father who dons armor preparatory to some enterprise to which the audience is not made privy.

The pattern of this act is typical; for a situation is set up; and, after most of the act has been given to various reactions to it, a sudden burst of action shifts the story forward. Passion, stoicism, pathos, joy, grief, ecstasy, cynicism, and farce are all demonstrated by turn; and the audience has been offered too much. Moreover, some of the speeches prevent the whole thing from being taken as a kaleidoscopic parody. Andrugio, the lovers, and Balurdo all belong to different worlds—to none of which the audience is expected to give full allegiance—but Marston seeks his understanding of the world in their coexistence and opposition. The best image of this is Mellida whose page-boy disguise deceives her father and her lover but is accidentally shattered by a nincompoop's twitching off her cap. The discovery is not fair, hardly tragic, and certainly not romantic; but it does suggest the awkward conflict of reality and illusion which bedevils ordinary living. If lovers would quit the mundane world and express themselves in a special language, a disdainful lad will bring them down to earth. The deliberate contrivances and the theatrical exploitation of them are more the work of the playwright who is entertaining his audience than of the dramatist who is carrying forward his argument. The dramatist exploits the situations as parts of a sequence of thematic development; the playwright exploits each one of them individually for its own end.

VI *Language and Poetic Style*

Variety of language and poetic style fascinated Marston. He took as much care with what literally was heard as he did with the staging of what was seen. The counterpoint of distinctive voices is always ingenious, and he took more care than his fellows in his orthography to catch inflexions, hesitations, and tones of speech. The rhetorical flights attempted by Piero, Andrugio, and Antonio are all variations on a stylistic theme. Balurdo's weak stretching after poetic effect—"I thinke, ha, ha, I think I shall tickle the Muses" (1.50)—is part of the "humour" of his character, but it is also one of a series of distinctive verbal sketches that includes Antonio's broken speech of grief, Piero's stuttering incoherence, Balurdo's continual, pitiful efforts to find the right word and his earnest pursuit of a wide vocabulary, even the move into Italian at a moment of passion.

This vivid interest in expression and language frequently leads Marston into Crispinine excess, even to confusion of meaning as he becomes almost drunk with language. "Marston often uses words as mere dabs of color, without much reference to their sense in the context; and when he cannot find one that happens to be of the right shade for its place in any one of his 'nocturns' in black or brown he rubs a few letters of the alphabet together and makes a new one."[3] Gustav Cross collected a very large list of such rubbings which proves that the risks of the procedure are outweighed by the rewards.[4] The rewards, if few, are genuine; for Marston's achievements in power and economy combine with realism. Moreover, the pointers he gives to a convincingly dramatic language were soon taken up by other dramatists.

As a whole, the play offers entertainment that slides disconcertingly from romantic melodrama to boisterous satirical comedy with hints of revenge tragedy. The audience is asked to sympathize and to laugh, to admire and to mock. Such a request is not an impossible one so long as there are clear indications of the response expected. A satirical extravaganza in which "it hath flow'd with the current of my humorous bloode, to affect (a little too much) to be seriously fantasticall" (1.2), as Marston wrote in dedicating the play to "No-body," *Antonio and Mellida* is an affected play by a very clever young man: it is fantastical certainly; but it also contains moments which deny laughter or scorn and which remind one that "seriously fantasticall" is a different thing from simply "fantasticall." G. K. Hunter argues that Marston "saw the world as a place where nobility is forever lapsing into caricature, and communication forever betraying intention."[5] It may well be that Marston's control of the means of dramatic communication betrayed this intention in *Antonio and Mellida:* his attempt to image the awkward clashes of feeling and event in the untrustworthy world of daily events by combining elements from comedy, satire, romance, farce, and tragedy failed because he lacked the necessary technical skills. In the second part of the history, he lets revenge tragedy color matters far more darkly.

VII Antonio's Revenge: *The Two-part Play*

Two-part plays were not unusual in Marston's time. In Harbage and Schoenbaum's *Annals of English Drama,* at least a dozen are recorded in the years 1597–99. Not all of these were planned as ten-act dramas in two parts; then, as now, sequels were sometimes written to take advantage of the popularity of a character or theme in a play originally intended to stand alone. Nonetheless, there are sufficient two-part plays to justify accepting the genre as a recognized one with its own dramaturgical problems. One solution to these is the use of a structural pattern first described by G. K. Hunter and called "dyptychal."[6] According to his pattern, the sequence of events in the two parts mirror each other:

Antonio and Mellida	*Antonio's Revenge*
Act 1	
The Genoese having been defeated by the Venetians, Piero triumphs and Antonio disappears.	Having killed Andrugio and dishonoured Mellida, Piero triumphs while Antonio despairs.

Act 2

| Antonio, disguised as an Amazon, reveals himself to Mellida; they plan to fly. | Antonio meets the imprisoned Mellida and resolves to fight Piero by dissimulation. |

Act 3

| Andrugio, exiled, with a price on his head, puts his trust in stoical fortitude. Antonio and Mellida flee from court. | The ghost of Andrugio commands Antonio to revenge. He charges him to fly from the court. |

Act 4

| Passion and stoical resolve alternate in both Andrugio and Antonio. Mellida is recaptured by Piero; Andrugio plans to recoup his fortunes by a final act of stoicism. | Antonio, disguised as a fool, contrasts his passion with the fool's invulnerability. Mellida is condemned by Piero and (by error) dies. Antonio and others plan a final revenge of Piero. |

Act 5

| Reconciliations in a masque. | Revenge achieved in a masque. |

Although Hunter's is a broadly conceived pattern, Marston possibly had it in mind while he was at work. There were good models of two-part plays on this plan for him to follow—Christopher Marlowe's *Tamburlaine* (alluded to jocularly in the Induction to *Antonio and Mellida*) and Shakespeare's *Henry IV*. Though Marston may have followed the dyptychal plan, there is no need to suppose that he ever thought that both parts would be produced as one performance; exigencies of time would have forbidden such staging, and no evidence exists elsewhere of the presentation of such double bills.

The Induction to *Antonio and Mellida* promised that a gracious acceptance of the play would result in a second part wherein certain characters "but slightly drawn" in the first would "receive more exact accomplishment." *Antonio's Revenge* can hardly have been the second part so envisaged when that promise was made. After witnessing what Antonio, not very convincingly, calls the "comick crosses of true love" in part one, the audience could not have expected the additional history to be so bloody and so calamitous as the second part became. Themes and situations from *Antonio and Mellida* are reenacted in horrific violence; follies become vices;

blustering threats are translated into acts of savagery. *Antonio's Revenge* opens with Feliche murdered, whereas the Induction had marked him for "more exact accomplishment." Piero and Antonio dominate the action. In the first part, they had not been "but slightly drawn"; in the second, they are virtually redrawn. Mellida is hardly heard from; the frivolous courtiers dwindle away; only Balurdo imperturbably survives and thereby is caused some awkwardness as he is swept into the violent revenge action. Marston's promise in the Induction is, therefore, an unusually misleading one, even for him.

VIII *Revenge Tragedy and Ritualized Horror*

Nonetheless, whatever may have been Marston's intentions, whatever the changes he made as he shaped his material, the two plays do tell one story, though the narrative is disorderly. *Antonio's Revenge* takes a direct and bloody line from savage murder and dishonor perpetrated by Piero to a brutal revenge made upon him by Antonio, Pandulpho (Feliche's father), and Alberto (Feliche's friend). The play hurtles into action with Piero—"unbrac't, his armes bare, smeer'd in blood, a poniard in one hand bloodie, and a torch in the other, Strotzo following him with a corde" (1.71),—exultant because of his murder of Feliche and his dishonoring of Mellida.[7] Such "festred rankling malice" had been hidden with a skill defying detection at the close of *Antonio and Mellida*.

After this beginning, the act moves through the quiet entry of Maria's party to reach a moment of stasis in the aubade sung at Mellida's window. This mood is interrupted by the shrill sound of Antonio's cornet and is then shattered by the discovery of Feliche's body at the window. Antonio's immediate reaction to Piero's furious denunciation of Mellida as unfaithful is bitter fury which has to crumble because of the seeming proof of Mellida's behavior and because of the news of Andrugio's death. The remainder of the act is about the impact of death upon the hearers, and it ends with a tableau in which everyone gathers to learn of the death and respond to the news. The overall pattern is very simple, reducing to quick, slow, quick, slow; the quick passages are loud and violent; the slow ones, quiet yet tense.

The violence and bloodshed are contained in a setting that suggests ritual, and much in the play reinforces the feeling that formality contains, and is being tested by, violence. Revenge tragedy provides Marston with the spectacular theatrical effects in which he delighted; but, as in *Antonio and Mellida*, although these effects give the

impression of a play surging forward with abundant incident, they are
actually set pieces that mark points in the debate that is the play's
central concern. In fact, Marston's handling of the conventions of
revenge tragedy is very much his own. The revenge taken during the
final masque has been criticized on the grounds that its savagery is
excessive and degenerates to tasteless silliness. The mode demanded
a vengeance that was as horrible as possible, and the time saw nothing
amiss in this occurrence. After the discovery of the Gunpowder Plot
in 1605, a special committee was struck to contrive hideous and
prolonged tortures for the conspirators. It was held proper that the
villain should suffer at least as much and, if possible, more than his
victims. This aspect of revenge tragedy appealed to the weaknesses as
well as strengths in Marston.

"At its worst, Marston's bent led him to futile extravagances of
passion and the empty inflation of character so marked in the later
Piero. His flair for strong scenes produced melodrama, stirring no
doubt on the Elizabethan stage but cold in the study."[8] Melodrama is
usually "cold in the study," but there is more to this criticism:
revenge tragedy called for extravagance that too easily became an
overplus. In the matter of masqued revenge, however, the theatrical
effect has particularly to be stressed. A masque—with its visual
splendors or ornate dress, with its stylized movement, and, above all,
with its music—lent the climactic act of revenge a special color. The
aural and visual patterns contained extravagant deeds of violence
without letting them seem ludicrous or excessive; indeed, they both
contained and heightened the effect of the final deeds. This
well-known fact helps explain the frequent masqued setting of the
tragic and bloody climax in seventeenth-century drama. In *Antonio's
Revenge* the torturing and killing of Piero, the last word in violence in
a play devoted to exploiting violence, is fitted into a ritual framework
and becomes the last and most impressive of a series of tableaux
during the action.

IX   *Musical Effects*

The dancing and chanting of the conspirators, their costumes, the
music—all ritualize the vengeance. In his fashioning of the conventions for a revenge tragedy, Marston relies often upon music. The
ghost of Andrugio is used to heighten the special atmosphere of the
culminating events by being "placed betwixt the musick houses" to
watch over events. The serenade and impassioned exchange of the
lovers under the girl's window is one of the oldest devices; and,

although tragedy adds a special poignancy, Marston, in the only scene where Antonio and Mellida appear together and are able to talk directly to each other (he is present during her trial, but is separated from her by his disguise as a fool), fits it bitterly to the mood of his play with great ingenuity. Mellida is not separated from him by the conventional balcony or garden lattice: she is in prison and talks with Antonio through the grating. The joy at meeting, the passionate exchanges, the unwillingness to part, are all twisted to this harsh setting. The whole scene looks forward to the love duet in *Il Trovatore* where, however, the hero is imprisoned. Marston's scene also has operatic elements which begin when Antonio alone disputes Senecan admonitions to patience. A series of disembodied voices is heard, in an almost surrealistic effect: a very imaginative moment:

MELL (within): Aye me.
ANT: And curse.
PANDULPHO (within): Black powers.
ANT: And cry.
MARIA (within): O heaven.
ANT: And close laments with————
ALBERTO (within): O me most miserable.
PANDULPHO (within): Woe for my deare deare sonne.
MARIA (within): Woe for my deare, deare husband.
MELLIDA (within): Woe for my deare deare love.
ANTONIO: Woe for me all, close all your woes in me . . .   (1.92)

The dialogue is a quintet in which four of the voices are offstage. The musical analogy is Antonio's own, for he says: "Come sigh againe, *Antonio* beares his part." When Mellida confesses her innocence, she is unaware of Antonio's presence until he takes her words and begins what may be called the duet of the lovers, a sadly brief one.

After these quasi-musical exchanges, the scene ends with actual music. Mellida leaves the grating, and Antonio breaks down and weeps (this act is not the futile reaction of a weakling as in the first part and so its fitness gives the moment a strong impact). Piero enters, gloats at this misery, and commands "some plaining dittie to augment despaire." The song's sense is contradicted by the intention behind it and by Piero's perverse enjoyment of it. The mood evoked by the music is at variance with that of the scene in which it is heard, as was the case with the aubade for Mellida.

The handling of music in this scene shows, at its most convincing, Marston's power to bend convention and to satisfy seemingly extradramatic requirements. The choir-boy actors had to have an opportunity to display their musical talents, and they do so here in necessary service of the drama. The song to assuage grief is an ordinary device (Marston uses it himself in *Antonio and Mellida* and in *The Malcontent*); and the overheard song that affects its intended and its accidental audience in different ways is also not new as Shakespeare's "Who is Silvia" proves. Marston fuses the two devices, and he so places the music that the poignancy of the song is enhanced and the surrounding ambivalent atmosphere is increased. The pattern of the scene is also interesting, for the movement is from a soliloquy through a quasi-musical chorus of grief to the anguished exchange of the lovers and the concluding song. The choric wailing of grief is yet another popular convention—the chorus of queens from Shakespeare's *Richard III,* a play Marston obviously knew well, comes at once to mind; but what Marston does is to orchestrate in a new way.

X   *The Actor and Acting as a Theme*

Against these skillful experiments must be placed some that fail. Antonio unconvincingly argues that he loves Julio's soul but must kill him because Piero's blood flows in his veins. The too-bloody stabbing of Julio, decorated by Antonio's overblown revenger's vaunting and grisly groans from beneath the stage, is too clearly a piece of grand guignol put in for its own sake. The part Balurdo plays presents a harder case for judgment, for he survives unchanged in his fatuity from part one. Often very amusing, his alienation from the dark activity in the court sets up resonances that add a distinctive note of unease to the general atmosphere. Occasionally, however, the note is so jarring that it cannot be resolved into the surrounding scheme. When Balurdo bustles on with only half his beard affixed and mutters about the shortcomings in the makeup department, he works outside the play. The role he sustains is a precarious one, and it illustrates the uncertain quality of the satire and humor in *Antonio's Revenge*.

The mockery takes its color from its surroundings and is dark. Balurdo struggles to make his distinctive voice heard; the other slight courtiers are barely discerned in the shadows; and, with Feliche dead, the voice of the sharply amusing satiric commentator is also silent. Antonio spurns the habit "of a spitting Critick" for the safer disguise of "a golden asse, a babl'd foole" (1.109). Piero himself eloquently supports Antonio's choice of his role in words which comment on both the foolery and the satire in the play:

> O, your unsalted fresh foole is your onely man:
> These vinegar tart spirits are too pearcing,
> Too searching in the unglewd joynts of shaken wits.
> Finde they a chinke, they'l wriggle in and in,
> And eat like salt sea in his siddowe ribs,
> Till they have opened all his rotten parts,
> Unto the vaunting surge of base contempt,
> And sunke the tossed galleasse in depth
> Of whirlepoole Scorne. Give me an honest fopp.
>
> (1.112)

Satiric themes gather around theatricalism—acting, copying, switching of roles, and changing of voices.

Reminders of the actor and his art appear throughout the play. As grand villain and deceiver, Piero's part, like Richard III's, constrains him to act all the time; and he relishes this fact. He enters enlarging on his skill at deception and calling for "lowde applause." He deserves it, for his performance at the discovery of Mellida's supposed falsity is superb. He delightedly gives himself cues when Andrugio's death is announced: "Dead, alas, how dead? [Give seeming passion.] / Fut weepe, act, faine. [aside] Dead, alas, how dead?" (1.81). Later, with Strotzo, he rehearses eagerly the trial scene, working out actions and lines which, when the scene is played, lead to actual death as Piero mingles acted rage with real contempt for his tool and strangles him. He can play the part bafflingly well; for, when told of Mellida's death, he confesses he is near to tears but he regains self-control, carries on with his wedding plans, and commands an exit in dignity to "lowdest musick," thereby leaving the audience in the theater to decide where pretense begins and ends in the speech.

In Piero's role as conceived by Marston of Machiavellian villain, Piero exhibits at times a tremendous passion which contrasts oddly with those displays which he deliberately affects. The one at Mellida's supposed infidelity is obliquely praised in Forobosco's anxious comment: "Keepe league with reason, gratious Soveraigne" (1.81). Were it not for Piero's unaffected outbursts, one might think that he despised such shows, hence his malicious efforts to jar Pandulpho from his stoic control. In contrast to the reactions of Antonio and Piero at the discovery of Mellida's behavior, Pandulpho merely laughs bitterly at his son Feliche's death and refuses to rage: "wring my face with mimic action; / Stampe, curse, weepe, rage, & then my bosom strike? / Away tis apish action, player-like" (1.83). These are awkward sentiments for a play so dependent upon player-like actions. Similarly, Antonio, some of whose outbursts are extravagant to the point of being ludicrous, can withdraw from passionate avowals to Mellida at her grating by saying, "Madam, I will not swell like a Tragedian, in forced passion of affected straines" (1.93). As Sir John Gielgud has remarked upon similar comments in *Hamlet*, "The advice to the players is always slightly embarrassing for the actor because he feels the audience is only waiting to catch him doing all the things he has told the players not to do . . . Shakespeare invites them to watch the actor who is playing the Prince discourse on acting and to see a play acted within a play."[9]

Some difficulties of interpretation are more easily solved, however, in *Hamlet* than in *Antonio's Revenge*. *Hamlet's* reflections about acting are a part of his personal discovery of what "seems," and they reveal something that is characteristic of him, as well as make a general comment about dramatic methods. They work directly for the play and encourage an audience's sympathetic response, for they are primarily *Hamlet's* reflections and not the author's. Comments in *Antonio's Revenge* are not restricted to one character, and they draw attention to the fact that the play is an illustration of dramaturgical philosophy, rather than a self-contained action that is valuable in itself and not merely as one example of the genus play. The audience is pulled in two ways, as it was in *Antonio and Mellida* and as it will be in Marston's later plays.

Marston has a tendency to experiment for experiment's sake rather than for the tragedy's or the comedy's sake. Because of his ceaseless experimentation and wry participation, his objective scanning of art combined with his subjective practice of it, he is a playwright's playwright. Since he writes passionately and dispassionately together, he generates a curious sense of involvement and detachment which, when it is contained within the play, creates the most powerful kind of satiric drama. An example of this achievement is the trial scene in which the devices of the disguise, the art of the actor, the tensions of the play-within-a-play, and the role of the fool and satirist in society are all brilliantly and dramatically debated. Thus, the innocent Mellida appears fittingly clad in white, but only by Piero's perverse order that "the strumpet in her bridall robes . . . may blush t'appear so white in showe, / And blacke in inward substance" (1.111). Antonio is present, but he is dressed in "a fooles habit with a little toy of a walnut shell, and sope, to make bubbles"

(1.109) and is giggling hideously throughout. Balurdo, who so clearly looks the fool he is, petulantly denies the character on the grounds that his appearance proves he is a courtier and gentleman. Piero directs the mockery of a trial: he acts as both judge and prosecuting counsel, and he pursues his own art of dissimulation to its height when he and Strotzo perform their playlet. Strotzo has no need to act the strangled man, for Piero slips from pretense to reality and actually does strangle him.

The sure handling of dramatic effect in such a trial scene only marks more sharply the uncertainty in the closing scenes of the play. Certain tendencies in Marston's argument have to contend against the powerful opposing pull of the revenge play convention. Piero's crimes are savagely punished, after which his exulting killers, amazingly, retire to "some religious order"; but they are praised as exemplars of the belief that "Calamity gives a man a steddy heart" (1.132). This stoic conclusion hardly follows from the play's bloody argument. Pandulpho had certainly voiced the stoic way when he asserted that "the gripe of chaunce is weake, to wring a teare, / From him that knowes what fortitude should beare" (1.83). He continues in this view for three acts and is never other than dignified in his cause, but Antonio takes from the first the contrary side in his pursuit of revenge:

> that griefe is wanton sick,
> Whose stomacke can digest and brooke the dyet
> Of stale ill relisht counsell. Pigmie cares
> Can shelter under patience shield: but gyant griefes
> Will burst all covert.
>
> (1.90)

Seneca is quoted only to be brutally dismissed as one "wrapt in furres . . . 'fore fiers" who "Forbidst the frozen Zone to shudder" (1.92).

Antonio's trenchant insistence on revenge convinces Pandulpho who breaks out in a speech that gains strength because its imagery is familiar from elsewhere in the play:

> Man will breake out, despight Philosophie.
> Why, all this while I ha but plaid a part,
> Like to some boy, that actes a Tragedie,
> Speakes burly words, and raves out passion:
> But, when he thinks upon his infant weaknesse,

He droopes his eye. I spake more then a god;
Yet am lesse than a man.

(1.121)

The debate between stoic endurance and passionate reaction is not
satisfactorily concluded; in fact, the conspirators drop it as they move
to their horribly bloody vengeance. Similarly, their retirement to
holy orders is hardly an imprimatur on their action. They withdraw
from a world whose ways they have learned, but the lesson cannot be
put into practice with any hope of reforming that world. They have
learned what to avoid rather than what to. do, and religion in this
instance is not a consolation but a metaphor; it merely conveniently
marks their withdrawal and, in a sense, Marston's from concluding
his debate authoritatively.

Some of the more serious passages in the play may lead one to
expect too much of what is, after all, a debate conducted within fixed
artificial artistic bounds. Much in revenge tragedy appealed to
Marston, for its power and ferocity matched a certain harshness in his
makeup. Its depiction of crime in a corrupt society fitted with his own
view of man's depravity. On the other hand, the plight of the
revenger, drawn to crush the finer side of his nature in order to
avenge the crime, isolated him in a foul society in much the same way
that the satiric commentator was isolated in his. The regular features
of the genre—bloody villain, vindictive ghost, stern avenger, sus-
penseful delays, incidental slaughters, and culminating bloodbath—
supplied ample opportunity for bold spectacle. At the same time,
traditions also allowed for stoic stances to be used. The images thus
presented harmonized with some traditional lines of Christian
thought—the fallen world of sinful man and the saint who endured
earthly temptation and horror in order to win salvation. These ideas
come together in revenge tragedy; and that they mix but do not
coalesce is part of the genre's fascination. The revenger is torn
between his inclinations to peace and his duty to perform violence: to
call his deed judicial murder begs the question that most occupies his
mind.

The plot leads inexorably in one direction; the tone of Marston's
argument in another; and, although the plot bends the tone to its own
conclusion, the climactic deed resolves only the plot, not the
argument. The debate focuses on what may be broadly called
neo-Stoic attitudes and their relevance to the revenge ethic. The
argument is exciting, even hectic, but no clinching statement

concludes it. Since Marston's philosophy was still evolving, he was trying to pin down what was real in the sense of what was both worthy and possible in a world in which imitation, forgery, illusion were prevalent. The theater provided him with a marvelously evocative image of this world as well as opportunity to probe its essence. The author, the actor, the role, and the audience provided a richly reflective mirror of the maze-like world of "real" life. Since the tension and interaction between this quartet helped shape his thinking and hence his plays, some general comment about Marston's attitude toward theatricality illuminates the ideas that he tried out in the two parts of *The Historie* and provides reference points for the plays yet to be studied.

XI   *Marston and the Idea of the Theater*

Marston looked on conventional forms with Sir Oliver Owlet's eye and was not scrupulous in his treatment of them: to adopt was to adapt. The early plays offer not so much the spectacle of a play by Marston as of the Marston who is writing a play. With him, it was often a case of "Tonight We Improvise" with the suspicion that he was not always fully in control of his improvisation. He is like a pianist who announces a Beethoven Sonata, begins to play it, and then wanders off into a Lisztian paraphrase on themes from the sonata. The music may be brilliant and exciting, but it can baffle and irritate those who had come to hear Beethoven. As for the critics, their problem is to decide what standards to use in addressing themselves to the paraphrase as a work of art. Thus in *The Historie*, the audience is offered something akin to a dramatic fantasie on themes suggested by revenge tragedy and the illusory arts of the theater. In *Antonio and Mellida*, the Italianate setting, the focus on court life, and the romantic plot with its evocation of every feeling from pathos to ridicule, all combine to push these motifs into the background. In *Antonio's Revenge*, however, motifs are kept relentlessly in the foreground until the bloodthirsty atrocities begin to dull by repetition or, worse, topple into the ludicrous. Revenge tragedy interests Marston and appeals to deep parts of his character, but it also awakens his cynical amusement and scorn.

Tragic involvement and sardonic detachment are immiscible; and one of Marston's discoveries is that, although this fact is logically true, it can be at times theatrically false. In modern terms, the absurd can become the serious and true. Marston continually explores this paradox in his drama. The art of the theater, its concern with and dependence upon illusion and imitation, its impositions upon the audience, the relationship between the actor and his part and the audience, all fascinate him. He probes the meaning of that simple phrase, "The play's the thing," and he does so not with the controlled scholastic objectivity of a Jonson but with a kind of wild, intuitive excitement. The appeal the theater had for him is possibly due to the fact that it deals with that conflict he knew in himself between involvement and detachment—that precarious balance between the impetus to a holy crusade against evil and an unholy delight in that crusade.

Marston tested the resilience of dramatic forms by guying them. He delighted in extravagant situations, extreme characters; as we have seen, he relished the artificiality of a play such as *Antonio and Mellida*, and, in its Induction, laid particular stress upon the fact that the actors were boys pretending to be men (and women). And yet, in the face of such obstacles, the play refuses to be simply unbelievable and ludicrous. This paradox Marston examines throughout his dramatic career in his own energetic, stimulating, but often disorderly manner. Drama sets up an unreal situation with actors pretending to be other people and induces the audience to accept these imposters and their imaginary problems as real.

One of the modern aspects of Marston's art is his concern with the actor, the audience, and the relationship between them. A reason for the impact of the current absurd and cruel theater is the playwrights' determination to reexamine the nature of this relationship. In discussions about theater and what is often too loosely called "anti-theater," "anti-theater" often seems to mean what would have been taken for a norm in Marston's time; that is, a vigorous and meaningful exchange between actor and audience—a simple realization that both were equally active components of the one artistic event, the performance of a play. Samuel Johnson stated very firmly and irrefutably what an audience did and did not believe in as it watched a play, and he inferred a relationship that Marston accepted, yet, characteristically, wished to test: "the delight of tragedy proceeds from our consciousness of fiction."[10] It is a debatable point, to say the least, how far Marston's audience was shocked or surprised by direct address from the stage and reminders of the fact that the play was an illusion. Modern theatrical modes are forcing spectators to reconsider this problem, but it is a perennial one which Elizabethan playwrights examined or commented upon in their own way. "What's Hecuba to him?" is a shrewd question, but a much harder one is: "What's Hamlet to him who asks 'What's Hecuba to him?'?"

Marston's plays debate this question continually. The Induction to *Antonio and Mellida* faces it boldly. "A frank confession of theatricalism is at the heart of the play's meaning" has written Martin Wine about *The Malcontent.* Marston, he continues, "would undoubtedly agree with those playwrights today who find in humor a source of creative liberty, for it is, in M. Ionesco's words, 'the intuition of the absurd': by dislocating the obvious, it is a means of disengaging us from ordinary perceptions and of forcing us to evaluate experience afresh. The evident theatrical humor of plays like *The Malcontent* turns plot into a dramatic metaphor of absurdity."[11]

Freedom of form or dislocation of the obvious is one way of looking at plots which might otherwise be seen as hectic and, at times, almost incoherent. But the present general argument is that the contradictions are deliberate; for, as G. K. Hunter suggests of *Antonio and Mellida,* "in the betrayal lies the art. The plot [of this play] is constructed as an extraordinary series of reversals, unprepared transitions from one level of experience to another (lower) one."[12] Certainly the characters switch personalities with dazzling speed; they surprise themselves as well as the audience: "As in Pirandello, the characters' lack of self-knowledge is ironically pointed to by a structure which presents this as symptomatic of the whole human condition."[13] Feliche and Balurdo, for instance, have "a conversation which proceeds entirely on lines of crossed connections, each speaker out of touch with the other."[14] Thus the characters are at odds with each other, the audience is at odds with them (deliberately contrived by Marston), and the two groups are played off against a third group, the actors, by means of Marston's reminders that the whole thing is only a play.

After Martin Esslin coined the term "Theatre of the Absurd," it was soon followed by others: Theater of Cruelty, Revolt, Anger, Shock. They were applied so arbitrarily that Esslin felt constrained to explain his intention in his original term. It was intended, he said, as "a working hypothesis, a device to make certain fundamental traits which seem to be present in the works of a number of dramatists accessible to discussion by tracing features they have in common. That and no more."[15] The value of terms such as "Theatre of the Absurd," or "comicall satyre," which was Jonson's excellent working hypothesis, lies in the comparisons they allow, not in the rules they are wrongly assumed to promulgate. Thus some plays by Jonson, Marston, John Webster, Cyril Tourneur, and others can be thought of as having certain traits in common without necessarily being considered mirror images of each other. They have a family likeness not only to themselves but to the Theatre of the Absurd insofar as they attend to similar fundamental issues of theatrical artifice. Marston's interest in these issues is so pronounced that comparisons between what he does and what some modern playwrights are doing are particularly striking.

Marston's insistence on reminding his audience that it is attending a stage performance, his parodistic intent, in a word, his Absurdism, have caused him to be compared of late with Luigi Pirandello, Eugene Ionesco, John Osborne, Samuel Beckett, and Peter Weiss among others. Comparisons of superiority, said Dr. Johnson, laid the foundations of lasting mischief; and one must certainly avoid taking these comparisons too naively and seeking to add to Marston's stature by hoisting him onto the shoulders of modern dramatists, since he can stand firmly on his own feet.

Nonetheless, considerations of his modernity are interesting not only for their own sake but for the light they throw upon certain fundamental aspects of the theatrical art which emerge as focal points of interest for both Elizabethan and modern dramatists. The talkers who bypass each other's meaning all the time are finely used in Ionesco's *The Bald Soprano,* but they are also to be found, talking just as absurdly, in *Gammer Gurton's Needle.* If the dislocation of plots is modern, it is also kin to the Elizabethan liking for a narrative which moved boldly from crisis to crisis and which worked in scenes rather than in a straightforward, logical sequence measured in acts. "Absurd" and "Absurdism" are valuable critical terms, but they describe a method which, if it has been daringly extended in recent years, is not entirely new.[16] The current vogue, however, should not allow Absurdism to be made the explanation of all Marston's successes and the excuse for all his failures.

XII   *Boys, Children and Adults as Actors*

Marston wrote his plays for the children's companies, and stress has lately been laid on the distinct effect upon the quality of Marston's plays that this actually must have had, especially on the satiric and grotesque parts. It is urged that the boys' stature and their squeaking voices would tend to shatter any tendencies to seriousness that there may be; that, as they are smaller than men, their attempts to imitate men naturally tend to be ludicrous. The ability of boys to mock adult behavior can lend something to the satire, but to apply the label of parodistic too widely to what they act is dangerous. It does not follow that all their acting is necessarily more mimicry than imitation.[17]

The words "boys" and "children" are misleading. In order to appreciate *Antonio and Mellida* and *Antonio's Revenge*, says Foakes, "we need to bear in mind that they were written to be acted by children, boys with piping voices from the choir school of St. Paul's Cathedral."[18] Visions of angelic, fair-haired boy sopranos are conjured up; the strong suggestion is of eight- or nine-year-olds rather than of boys in their early teens (Solomon Pavy was "scarce thirteen" when he died, and Field was acting in *Poetaster* when he was fourteen). The choirboys were trained musicians, and their voices could be used in choirs until they broke (generally around the age of fifteen or sixteen years): indeed, the break in a choirboy's voice can be disguised for some time in his singing. The actors of Marston's plays were not, therefore, necessarily little children. The use of words like "juvenile" or "adolescent" would perhaps be more accurate, and Marston was well aware of the quality of his actors, for the image of the actor, on the stage and off it, continued to excite his imagination. The potentialities of the image are explored in all his plays.

XIII What You Will

The setting, the themes, and many of the characters of *What You Will* are familiar from the verse satires. The setting is Venice where "naughtes knowne but by exterior sence" (2.252) and where only the rare man can hang onto that "deere unbeleefe" which "anchorst him from floting with the tide of vulger faith" (2.269). In an unpleasant way, "tis now the age of gold, For it all marreth and even virtues sold" (2.263). The themes are greed for money, the confusing of love and lust, the aimless pursuit of luxury, and the general malaise this behavior breeds. There is ample scope for Marston the satirist here: Marston the dramatist tries to accommodate this material in a plot that is rich in comic invention and in the situations that he loved to exploit.

In the main plot, one which abounds in disguises, crossings, and misunderstandings, Albano, a wealthy merchant, has been presumed drowned; and his widow, Celia, deciding to marry again, has chosen Laverdure, an extremely clothes-conscious, impoverished knight. To prevent this marriage, Iacomo, a rejected suitor, and Andrea and Randolpho, the brothers of Albano, dress up Francisco, a performer who looks and even stutters like Albano when angry, as Albano. Laverdure learns of the plot, and he tells Celia that he plans to dress up a fiddler as yet another Albano to baffle the plotters. Thus, when Francisco-Albano and the real Albano (who has, of course, escaped drowning) arrive atogether at Celia's and demand entry, she mocks both of them as imitations (Laverdure's protestations that he never did put his fiddler idea into practice are brushed aside). Eventually, an appeal is made to the Duke, confusions are cleared up, and everyone sets out for a night of celebration.

The first act, which shows the manner in which the satirist and the dramatist work together, opens with "Enter *Quadratus*, *Phylus* following him with a lute, a Page going before *Quadratus* with a torch." Any thoughts that Quadratus, a cynical gallant, is the lover going to serenade his lady are quickly dispelled; for Phylus, Iacomo's page, appeals to him to reclaim the wits of his master who is mad for love. Quadratus, in Mercutio-like vein, mocks these feelings until Iacomo enters, "unbraced and careles drest." He is a richly romantic lover who rhapsodizes about love and ignores Quadratus's tart comment that "hee's madde most palpable, / He speaks like a player, hah! poeticall" (2.238). Iacomo's love vaporings are brushed aside by Quadratus, who suggests that love is the "abject out-cast of the world" and that, as society now scorns old values and virtues, it is safer to "love onely hate." Iacomo is heedless; and, as he falls to swearing that he will "make charmes" to prevent the forthcoming marriage of his love, Celia, Quadratus leaves in amused disgust. Iacomo has his page sing a serenade. There is no response. The serenade is repeated "and is answered, from above a Willow garland is floung downe and the songe ceaseth." This scorn fires Iacomo to thoughts of revenge and he menacingly asks in conventional manner, "What rage so violent as love turn'd spight?" (2.240).

At this melancholic juncture, Randolfo and Andrea, who are as upset as Iacomo about Celia's projected marriage to the upstart Laverdure, enter with a petition against the marriage which they propose to offer to the Duke. The movement of the action falters as the wretchedness of the world becomes the theme of general conversation of a cynical kind. Iacomo abandons the role of romantic and scorned lover for that of the cynic and the railing critic. One moment Iacomo lyrically extols love and at the next denounces it as a hypocritical passion roused only by dreams of greed:

> O ill-nurs'd custome! no soner is the wealthy
> Marchant dead,
> His wife left great in faire possessions,
> But giddie rumor graspes it twixt his teeth
> And shakes it bout our eares. Then thether flock
> A rout of crased fortunes whose crakt states
> Gape to be sodderd up by the rich masse
> Of the deceased labores, and now and then
> The troupe of *I beseech and protest!*
> *And beleeve it sweete,* is mix'd with two or three
> Hopefull, well stockt, neat clothed *Cytizens.*

> (2.242)

These are not ill-made verses, but they come a little unexpectedly from the erstwhile Romeo. Marston may have meant a development in character to give credence to them, but all that results is an abrupt change. Nonetheless, Iacomo maintains the role and plays it well.

The grumbling of the three men is interrupted by the cornets of "*Lorenze Celso* the loose *Venice* Duke," who makes night his day and day night. "*Enter the Duke coppled with a Lady, two copples more with them, the men having tobacco pipes in their hands, the woemen sitt, they daunce a round. The Petition is delivered up by Randolfo, The Duke lightes his tobacco pipe with it and goes out dauncing*" (2.244). Comic invention replaces satiric commentary; the trio of petitioners gives over their castigations of society and the serious pretensions of their attitudes; and they concoct a comical plan to undo Celia's proposed marriage.

Such changes of pace are typical of the act. Individual moments and events, speeches in various scenes are all effective; but they are not necessarily those of the characters for whom one would think they had been planned. For example, Quadratus has the role of cynic at the start, but his place is then taken by the brothers and Iacomo. Equally disturbing is the suggestion of the close relationship between Quadratus and Iacomo, for after this scene they have very little to do with each other. Celia is quite cleverly kept offstage during the first act, and she remains offstage during the next two acts as well. The suspicion rises that her existence is something of an excuse for exploiting certain attitudes and speeches on the part of others. The exhibition by the Duke illustrates the thesis that court life is corrupt, and the tableau represents the kind of life which the three men have been castigating. The smoking and dancing band of idlers is an effective piece of theater, but the contribution of the scene to the play

is momentary. The Duke is scarcely heard of again, and he is not seen
until the end of the play when entanglements are unwound and when
all join with him in a night of what is clearly cheerful revelry rather
than the lascivious wastrel life represented in the first act. The first
appearance of the Duke's party evokes an atmosphere and setting
which is not used thereafter.

XIV   *The Satiric Themes of the Play*

The first act presents a body of lively comment upon marriage,
widows, and wealth that is laced with some theatrically exciting
moments; but these parts are more interesting than the whole act.
But when these slightly clumsy preliminaries are over, Marston the
satirical dramatist develops the main plot. He dramatizes the motif of
the clothes-mad world through the concern of various characters
with clothes: this is made, for instance, a particular aspect of Albano's
character:

> O I shall nere forget how he went cloath'd
> He would maintaine't a base ill us'd fashion
> To bind a Marchant to the sullen habit
> Of precise black, cheefly in *Venice* state
> Where Marchants guilt the top.
> . . . .
> Me thinkes I see him now how he would walke:
> With what a jolly presence he would pace
> Round the *Rialto*.

(2.241)

Here again a mellowing is noticed in Marston's attitude: Albano is
allowed fine clothes because he can afford them; moreover, they are
tasteful, they match his generous nature, and it is fitting that he
should wear them. When the poseur dresses gaudily in the hope of
being taken for such a man as Albano, he is attacked; and Laverdure is
such a man. His clothes too brashly speak the man and he merits such
an attack. In the first scene of act 2, the introductory stage direction
reads: "One knockes: *Laverdure* drawes the Curtaines sitting on his
bed apparalling himselfe, his trunke of apparaile standing by him"
(2.245). He sends his boy to see what the visitors are wearing, rather
than who they are, and he allows them entrance on hearing they are
well dressed. Hastily, he sets the scene for them: "My gold-wrought
Wast-coate and Night-cap, open my Trunck, lay my richest sute on

the top, my Velvet slippers, cloth of gold gamashes, where are my cloth of silver hose . . ." Unfortunately, the hose are at the pawnshop; and he has to make do with a display of "my richest Gloves, Garters, Hatts, just in the way of their eyes" (2.245). The satire is visual and dramatic, and it is legitimate because of Laverdure's character.

A little later, when Francisco is being dressed as Albano, Marston has an opportunity for more commentary about the illusions bred by dress. When the man dresses, Marston takes typical care with the directions: "Enter *Francisco* halfe drest, in his black doublet and round cap, the rest riche, *Iacomo* bearing his hatte and feather, *Andrea* his doublet and band, *Randolfo* his cloake and staffe, they cloath *Francisco*, whilst *Bydet* creepes in and observes them. Much of this is done whilst the Acte is playing" (2.260). As plotters fuss about Francisco, Iacomo, now firm in his role as the satiric commentator, remarks:

> I warrant you, give him but faire riche cloathes,
> Hee can bee tane, reputed any thing,
> Apparail's growne a God and goes more neate
> Makes men of ragges, which straight he beares aloft,
> Like patcht up scar-Crowes to affright the rout
> Of the Idolatrous vulgar, that worship Images.
>
> (2.260)

Even more closely knit into the play are Albano's comments about marriage and love when he returns to find his wife so soon thinking about another marriage, for his views spring directly from his nature and his situation. His dismay grows into incredulity and thence to more familiar but characteristic disgust. Love, he reckons, has gone out of fashion:

> But O tis growne a figment: love a jest:
> A commick Poesie: the soule of man is rotten
> Even to the core; no sound affection.
> Our love is hollow-vaulted, stands on proppes
> Of circumstance, profit or ambitious hopes.
>
> (2.263)

Albano has a right to say this, his character and his mood make it apt to him and only secondarily a satiric speech. Furthermore, the mood is controlled; he is angry but not ludicrously vehement. Perhaps best of all, when he is despised and rejected by family and friends who keep insisting that he is not the real Albano, he is so furious that he can almost believe that he is indeed not himself; but he speaks against that persistent Marstonian target, Opinion:

> Doth not *Opinion* stamp the currant passe,
> Of each mans valew, vertue, quality?
> Had I ingross'd the choice commodities
> Of heavens trafike, yet reputed vile
> I am a rascall; O deere unbeleefe,
> How wealthy dost thou make thy owners wit?
> Thou traine of knowledge, what a priviledge
> Thou giv'st to thy possessor: anchorst him,
> From floting with the tide of vulger faith:
> From being dam'd with multitudes deere unbeleefe.

(2.269)

Marston here achieves what previously had eluded him, a fine and trenchant irony; for motive, behavior, and speech are in accord.

By unwitting irony, the discussions of and the display of different sorts of satire in scenes dominated by Quadratus and Lampatho are less closely woven into the play's structure. The subplot is more in the nature of scenes in which aspects of satire are discussed and illustrated. Quadratus, an epicure, and Lampatho Doria, a discontented scholar ready to kick over the traces, are the main voices of the satiric discussion. Quadratus is articulate and imaginative, fanciful and brilliant in argument; but he is essentially an elusive character. He is the commentator and voice of reasonableness in the action, but he is not always the voice of reason or morality.

For example, Quadratus's appeal is not unquestioned, for his eloquent arguments at different times in the play do not harmonize with each other. He would rescue Lampatho from the cloistered scholar's cell and have him exchange the musty fopperies of books for the reality of everyday life. In the end, however, he would have him accept the cynical, live-and-let-live, greedy Venetian world, have him realize what the worth of opinion is, but float nonetheless with its lazy tide. In a series of lively episodes, he irritates Lampatho into entering the everyday Venetian world but refuses to allow him, or the theater audience, the comforts of the expected moral sanctions. The different points of view that Quadratus expresses suggest he is that useful figure, the sensible man in disguise who undermines a corrupt society from within: unfortunately, such expectations are dashed when, at the end, he refuses to doff his 'disguise' but elects to join that society. The play itself swerves with him at this point. In act 1, the Duke and his courtiers entered to make a tableau as it were of the venal, luxurious society; at the end of the play, the same people and society are represented as cheerful and satisfying.

Many a gay bustling comedy ends with such general merrymaking, but few spend the time that *What You Will* does suggesting the darker side of such living: the native hue of comedy is chastened by such satiric casts of thought. In performance, however, the awkwardness of Quadratus's stances could be merged into a generally cheerful comic action (some judicious cutting, it must be admitted, would help). Quadratus opens the play and closes it, and he ranges from the tart observer of love-sick Iacomo to the cheerful lyricist of "Musick, Tobacco, Sack and Sleepe, / The tide of Sorrow backward keepe" (2.252).

Lampatho's recognition of the futility of his protracted studies strikes the corresponding serious note. Lampatho is the butt; yet, at the end of act 3, when he is led in his melancholy to question the worth of his years of book-study and seclusion from life in the drudge's way to knowledge, he has the finest speech in the play, one which in an oblique manner counterpoints that of Albano. Both men discourse on the theme of real knowledge. Lampatho, in making the speech, sounds a deeply personal and convincing note; he is a different Lampatho from the man seen in other scenes: the sharp-tongued railer becomes a quizzical, philosophic, and very sympathetic man:

> *Delight* my spaniell slept, whilst I bausd leaves,
> Tossd ore the dunces, por'd on the old print
> Of titled wordes, and stil my spaniell slept.
> Whilst I wasted lampoile, bated my flesh,
> Shrunk up my veines, and still my spaniel slept.
> And still I held converse with *Zabarell*,
> *Aquinas, Scotus,* and the musty *sawe*
> Of antick *Donate,* still my spaniell slept:
> Still went on went I, first *an sit anima,*
> Then and it were mortall, O hold! hold!
> At that they are at braine buffets fell by the eares,
> A maine pell mell togither—still my spaniell slept.

> (2.257–58)

In the remainder of the play, Marston busily tries his hand at various theatrical effects. When Celia and her attendant women are introduced in act 4, they are, conventionally enough, discussing men, but, unconventionally, they do so while they play shuttlecock. The fact that the actors are boys is the excuse for a lively but irrelevant classroom scene and, later, for a mock court where the boys do mimic adults. The tricking of Simplicius in this scene by one of the boys dressed as a girl forms a skit on the main plot's concern with such tricks, but its direct relevance to the main action is slight.

Basically, the structure of the play is slack. The main plot is good, but, characteristically, it is rushed through and its implications and possibilities are not fully developed. Whenever Quadratus and his group intrude upon events, the forward movement falters. *What You Will* is clearly a play first and a satire second. Crowded with incident and attractive ideas, the quality is enough to outweigh the unsteadiness of the hand that controls them. A clearer grasp of dramatic techniques and a better understanding of the necessities of dramatic management can be discerned.

Marston's interest in staging and in opportunities offered by the theater grows apace. The Duke's smoking party and the dances, the shuttlecock scene, the love-song scene with its mysterious garland, the dressing-up scene—all are effective, even when they stand apart from the main flow of the action. Openings of the second and third acts have been mentioned, and that of the third is particularly interesting for Marston's having action accompanied by music— Bydet spies on the plotters and then runs off to reveal it to the would-be dupes. Music before the last act is also made to serve a double purpose—it is both the inter-act music and the dinnertime entertainment for the little banquet which opens that act.

XV   *The Apprentice Achievement*

In their various ways, *What You Will* and the other plays so far examined are apprentice works in which Marston tries different methods of combining satire with, chiefly, comic action. The craft is slowly being learned, not only the fusing of satire into the action but also the controlling of the play as a form in itself. Marston's chief clog, perhaps, is in trying to do too much. He packs a great many things into his plays; he uses the stage inventively and ingeniously; but, as in his satires, an abundance of irregularly controlled material confuses his form and overall design.

The plays are not of great merit, but not one of them lacks interesting or effective scenes. All of them contain good speeches;

and, although these lines are not always spoken by the right person or at the proper time, the speaker, the moment, and the speech happily coincide occasionally. But, if the satirist occasionally elbows the dramatist aside, the playwright is the dominant figure. In these comedies, the likeness to plays and the withdrawal from satire are noticeable. These comedies are full of situations and ideas awaiting development, both by Marston and by his contemporaries.

CHAPTER 6

The Malcontent

THE early history of *The Malcontent* is obscure. It was first published in 1604, in which year three separate editions of the play appeared. The second edition corrected some errors in the first and added a Prologue and Epilogue, and the third added not only an Induction written by John Webster, but also considerable extra material by Marston: this last edition was the text used by the King's Men at the Globe. It seems that the play originally was acted by the children of the Queen's Revels and was acquired subsequently by the King's Men, ostensibly in retaliation on the children's taking one of their plays, possibly *The Spanish Tragedy*.[1] The Induction introduces leading actors from the King's Men who make some fleeting allusions to this affair (it was apparently widely enough known not to need much explanation) as they discuss the play's type and what has been done to adapt it to their theater.[2]

The adaptation consisted of new dialogue to offset some of the music that had to be pruned from the production. The children's companies utilized their musical training by embellishing their productions with a good deal of music, not only during the play, but in between the acts and even as an overture to the play. The adult companies in the public theaters were not niggardly in their musical offerings, but they could not match the scope of the children.

I "An Enterlude Called the Malecontent, Tragicomoedia"

In taking *The Malcontent,* the King's Men obviously hoped that it would draw crowds and make money. Marston's reputation, and possibly prior performances of the play, had attracted the attention of what Cundall, in the Induction, called "discontented creatures" who "wrest the doings of any man to their base malitious appliment." Cundall also denied that *The Malcontent* is a bitter play by claiming somewhat too ingenuously that "tis neither Satyre nor Morall, but the meane passage of a historie" (1.142). Marston himself is more forthright in his address "To the Reader": "I have not glanced at disgrace of any, but of those, whose unquiet studies labor innovation, contempt of holy policie, reverent comely superioritie, and establisht unity: for the rest of my supposed tartnesse, I feare not, but unto every worthy minde it will be approved so generall and honest, as may modestly passe with the freedome of a Satyre" (1.139). The entry in the Stationers' Register describes it as "An Enterlude called the Malecontent, Tragicomoedia."

The play is all of these things, for it plunders all the popular genres of the day for material. To satire, morality, history, and tragicomedy could be added domestic tragedy, romantic comedy, and, especially, revenge tragedy. Revenge supplies so much of the material and so affects the mood that *The Malcontent* might well be called "revenge comedy," for such a paradoxical description suits its peculiar and powerful attractions. Murder, lust, violence, hypocrisy, and corruption are its dark ingredients, but they are contained within and controlled by a well-organized comic structure. This structure is that of a disguise plot. At its heart is Altofronto, sometime Duke of Genoa, who, in his disguise as Malevole, the malcontent, conspires to win back his dukedom from the usurping Duke Pietro and Mendoza, the latter having used Pietro as only a tool to further his own ambitions for the dukedom. Malevole's skillful manipulations eventually open Pietro's eyes to his own weakness and to the wickedness of Mendoza whose cunning plots only bring about his own downfall: Altofronto then reassumes his ducal power.

Evil purposes are thwarted; there are dangers but no deaths. But, if the structure is that of comedy, its working out is not straightforwardly comic. *The Malcontent* is as much a problem comedy as Shakespeare's *Measure for Measure* or *All's Well That Ends Well*. As a satiric comedy, it has a firmer organization than Shakespeare's problem comedies by virtue of its focus upon a dominating central character. This concentration means, however, that *The Malcontent* is Malevole's play; and it is strong or flawed as he is strong or flawed as a dramatic character. The play concerns Altofronto's successful regaining of his dukedom, but it is properly named after his assumed character of Malevole. The nature of Malevole's character and that of the relationship between the characters of Malevole and Altofronto create the problem of Marston's comedy. Characteristically, Marston focuses his drama upon an ambiguous controlling figure.

One of Marston's most aggravating problems in dramatizing satire was how best to handle the figure of the satiric commentator. In *The Malcontent*, he solves the problem brilliantly and, on the face of it, simply. The commentator, instead of being introduced to annotate the scene and possibly to take an occasional direct part in the action, is the hero of the play who no longer intrudes on other persons' stories but acts out his own. Some parts of the commentator's character, however, are elusive; others are contradictory beyond the plain explanation of sobriety's assuming the cloak of wildness. One cannot always be sure of how much Altofronto is acting a role, for Marston's dexterity with the metaphor of acting in this play is bewildering. To achieve his ends, Altofronto disguises himself, and the essentially theatrical nature of this device cannot be overemphasized. Altofronto is both actor and producer, even author, of his own play; many of those around him move at his dictate or perform under his scathing direction. He lives in a world of sham and hypocrisy, an actor in a world of actors.

Most of the major characters assume a disguise or dissemble at one time or another. Fittingly, Altofronto's archenemy, Mendoza, is a masterful actor; and he is so grandly ironic in his contempt for everyone else and in his delight in his seeming ability to deceive them that he says, after gulling Pietro: "Who cannot faine friendship, can nere produce the effects of hatred" (1.160). He believes himself not only to be the best actor but the only one. To celebrate the apparent success of his plans, he orders a play: "any quicke done fiction . . . some far fet tricke, good for Ladies, some stale toy or other . . . tis but for a fashion sake, / Feare not it shall be grac'd man, it shall take" (1.207–8). The irony, and ultimately the source of the comedy in the action, is that he is unwittingly caught up in just such a "far fet tricke" and becomes merely a character in Altofronto's play rather than the deviser of his own.

In *The Malcontent*, Marston deliberately plays off quickly done fictions, farfetched tricks, stale toys, and fashionable devices against harsh realities and recognizable attitudes and emotions. The material and the basic approach are strongly reminiscent of *The Historie of Antonio and Mellida*, but the control is firmer with the result that the tired metaphor of life's a stage and men are but players is infused with invigorating comic life. The plot brashly urges its theatricality, and it is melodramatic in its reliance upon the very long arm of coincidence and upon strange chances. Marston uses *The Malcontent* to explore still further the artifice of the theater and its implications; and his plot, character, and meaning are shaped by this exploration. The obviousness of the contrivances only makes the pungent "reality" exuded by the play the stronger.

Marston was always aware of how much his plays stood to lose in reading as compared with the result of their stage performance. The danger was never greater than in *The Malcontent:* "onely one thing afflicts me, to thinke that Scaenes invented, meerely to be spoken, should be inforcively published to be read" (1.139). Those who could not see *The Malcontent* "presented with the soule of lively action" might misinterpret his meaning and possibly be "conscious of contradiction, irrelevance and repetition, where a theatre-goer would experience ironic reversal, sequential underscoring and dramatic emphasis."[3]

II *The Action of the Play*

As the play opens, "The vilest out of tune Musicke being heard" is coming from Malevole's chamber. Malevole is not seen, but his foul abuse of the listening courtiers mingles with the discordant music. Pietro calls him "a man or rather a monster . . . his highest delight is to procure others vexation . . . his speach is halter-worthy at all howers: I like him faith, he gives good intelligence to my spirit, makes me understand those weakenesses which others flattery palliates" (1.146). This assessment is true, but in ways of which Pietro does not dream; one strand in the action is to be the rigorous, even savage, education in understanding his weaknesses which he is to receive from his teacher.

When Malevole enters, he rends the court in terms familiar from the verse satires as "dreames, dreames, visions, fantasies, *Chimeras,* imaginations, trickes, conceits" (1.148). Left alone with Pietro, Malevole waxes even more intemperate as he discovers to the Duke that his wife, Aurelia, and Mendoza are lovers. He elaborates his message so sickeningly that Pietro's horrified retort, "Hydeous imagination," might be as well applied to Marston, the author, as to Malevole, his creation. Pietro leaves threatening revenge. Malevole's character having been limned in the most revolting outline, it is now revealed that he is disguised and that his vicious malcontent is a pose. He is neither a mere ranter nor an idly sadistic tale-bearer; he is a revenger who is working with a deeper purpose and for an unusual aim: *"The hearts disquiet is revenge most deepe./ He that gets blood, the life of flesh but spilles, / But he that breakes hearts peace, the deare soule kills"* (1.150).

Altofronto ends his soliloquy by asserting that: *"Beneath God naught's so deare as a calme heart."* Pietro will learn this truth, but it becomes more uncertain as to whether Altofronto speaks from knowledge of possession or of loss.

The audience only learns Malevole's true name and the details of his history when the faithful Celso enters and calls him "My honor'd Lord" (1.151). Celso urges violent action, but not even the remembrance of his faithful wife, Maria, who is imprisoned in the Citadel, can shake Altofronto's resolve to let the discord in the court work its own confusion. His sober admonition to restraint strikes home with redoubled force when set against the loud vituperation which a moment ago was being thrown in the face of Pietro and his court. It is still further heightened when Celso and Altofronto are interrupted by Bilioso and "Malevole shifteth his speach" (1.152) into his original taunting vein.

The shifting of voices here dramatically emphasizes the theme of the deceptiveness of appearance. Two men speak but the raging malcontent and the calm aristocrat are indistinguishable to the spectator's eye. This changeableness carries to the other characters. Thus Mendoza first enters "with three or foure sutors" to whom he grandly, yet offhandedly, promises his seemingly infallible aid: "Leave your suites with me, I can and will" (1.153). His portrait is that of the masterful politician. Brusquely dismissing Malevole, he falls into a soliloquy about the delights of being a court favorite and the lover of the Duchess Aurelia. When he hurries away to compose a sonnet to her charms, he leaves the false impression that he is a rather unpleasant variety of Inamorato Curio.

The entry of the ladies of the court dramatizes an old theme from *The Scourge of Villanie,* for they demonstrate lust in action when their price—of jewels and of money—is paid openly. Ferneze buys Macquerelle's voice to urge his suit to Aurelia and frustrate Mendoza's. So, when Mendoza returns murmuring what he is pleased to call "passionate flashes" from his sonnet, Aurelia coldly dismisses him. At once he quits his fawning idiocy and attacks women in a fierce tirade that refutes his previous panegyric. In the midst of it, Pietro rushes in, sword in hand, to kill Mendoza. The play is full of such effective entries, but none is more crushingly met:

PIE: A mischiefe fill thy throate, thou fowle jaw'd slave;
            Say thy prayers.
MEN: I ha forgot um.

(1.158)

Such aplomb deflates Pietro. Mendoza turns his wrath against Ferneze and coolly produces a plan whereby Ferneze will be surprised in Aurelia's room and cut down by Mendoza as he flees. When Aurelia arrives, she will find Mendoza seemingly holding Pietro back from her lover. This act will win Mendoza her friendship, and any revenge she plans against Pietro will be confided in Mendoza and relayed by him to Pietro.

Act 2 shows Marston's stagecraft at its boldest as he reworks, in his own highly colored way, the scene from Thomas Heywood's *A Woman Killed With Kindness* in which Frankford surprises his wife with Wendoll. Heywood's scene is fine, somber, and restrained with no bloodshed; Frankford's one sudden loss of control is swiftly countered; but the passion and grief are no less strong for being mastered. Marston, who seeks melodramatic action as well as tragic passion, crowds his act with wild event. His dark night is filled with furtive talk and with disturbing noises. Ferneze slips to his assignation watched by a gloating Mendoza. That this is a scene of lust with no tinge of romantic adventure to it is emphasized by the coarse gossip of Maquerelle and her cronies. Another aspect is shown when Pietro reluctantly approaches with his bodyguard to apprehend the adulterers. His frame of mind is close to Frankford's; but, unlike him, Pietro receives only hypocritical encouragement from Mendoza and cynical gibes from Malevole. The talk of Maquerelle's group that concerns old wives' nostrums for aphrodisiacs swells grossly again.

Cutting across this background of casual court lechery and despair, the langorous strains of a love song coming from Aurelia's room are now heard: all the evocations of romantic love called up by this music are at variance with the discordant scene in which it is set. Indeed, "Whilst the Song is singing, enter *Mendoza*, with his sword drawne standing readie to murder *Ferneze*" (1.169). The gentle music marks an uneasy lull that is shattered by uproar within the Duchess's apartments. All goes off exactly as Mendoza had promised it would, and he crowns his performance by audaciously assuming the role of the honest man beguiled in a vicious world. He woos Aurelia in the manner that Richard III wooed Anne:

O God, O God, how we dull honest soules,
Heavie braind men, are swallowed in the bogs
Of a deceitfull ground, whilest nimble bloods,
Light jointed spirits spent, cut good mens throats,
And scape. Alas, I am too honest for this age.

(1.171)

Her reaction to this speech is splendidly ironic. She humbly apologizes for misunderstanding him, lays plans at once to murder Pietro, and leaves; and Mendoza coolly congratulates himself about his "prosperous trecherie." Malevole enters and is told to get rid of Ferneze's body. Marston then caps this act with one more startling effect: Ferneze, long lying almost forgotten, a mere body, groans and is seen to be alive. Only Malevole takes this for granted and greets him with superb coolness: "Hark, lust cries for a surgion, what news from Limbo?" (1.173). After making a rather formal speech about the sinfulness of lust, Malevole helps Ferneze away into hiding.

Pietro takes no satisfaction in the proof of his wife's faithlessness. Word of it is sent to her father, the Duke of Florence, whose support, vital to Pietro's retaining the dukedom, is likely to be withdrawn on receiving it. This news, plus that that the common people are stirring against Pietro, encourages Malevole to hope that Fortune is turning his way; and this hope is confirmed when he is hired by Mendoza to kill Pietro. Mendoza expects to succeed Pietro; and, with him dead and with Aurelia discredited, he plans to consolidate his position by marrying Maria, Altofronto's "widow" whom he holds prisoner. By hiring Malevole, he makes his ruthless intrigues mere paper dragons; but his cold-bloodedness and drive remain impressive: Marston allows the audience to see that he cannot succeed, but does not thereby reduce him to the stature of a fool. Malevole reveals the extent of Mendoza's duplicity to an incredulous Pietro who assumes a hermit's disguise and returns to court to announce his own death.

Meanwhile, the court seethes with gossip about Ferneze and Aurelia; but she is "as one confirmed in her owne vertue against ten thousand mouthes that mutter her disgrace" and is "presently for daunces" (1.187). Aurelia sweeps in and, to the horror and grudging admiration of the courtiers, insists upon beginning the dancing. The emotional atmosphere becomes more and more highly charged as the music plays, the stage swirls with the movement of dancers, and messengers frantically seek the Duke who now enters and, in a set piece, describes his own death. Mendoza presses on swiftly; he banishes Aurelia and sends Malevole to plead his case to the imprisoned Maria. The Hermit (Pietro) he then hires to poison Malevole. The latter, returning for authority to enter the prison, is sent back with additional orders to poison the Hermit.

Before Pietro can assimilate this mounting villainy, Aurelia passes on her way to banishment. The suddenness of her fall has plunged her into despair, and, in Marston's conventional reversal, she is shocked into complete repentance. Malevole, with seeming callousness, cuts short Pietro's delight at his wife's change of heart and rises to his most savage denunciation of man as he relentlessly goads Pietro: "this earth is the only grave and *Golgotha* wherein all thinges that live must rotte: tis but the draught wherein the heavenly bodies discharge their corruption, the very muckhill on which the sublunarie orbes cast their excrement: man is the slime of this dongue-pit, and Princes are the governours of these men" (1.197).

Pietro is forced to recognize his own particular sins rather than rest in delight at Aurelia's recovery and in just horror about Mendoza's wickedness. He dedicates himself, therefore, to "restoring Altofront to regency" (1.197). This vow is Malevole's cue to reveal his true identity: Celso and Ferneze enter, and the four men "cloase to counsell" as "the time growes ripe for action" (1.198). Meanwhile, Malevole himself is to be further tested; as the bearer of Mendoza's offers to Maria, he must watch as she treats them with such contempt, with such virtue, as tries him to the extreme: "O God, how loathsome this toying is to mee" (1.204). He, like Pietro, must endure harsh trial; for no one is exempt.

The concluding scene is set at court where the masque, ordered by Mendoza to celebrate his accession to power, is awaited. Against the background of the courtiers' lascivious chatter, Maria refuses a last personal offer by Mendoza; sentence of death is forestalled by the masque itself, whose dancers gradually surround Mendoza before unmasking themselves. He abjectly begs for life, which Altofronto grants contemptuously: "Hence with this man: an Eagle takes not flies" (1. 215); and Mendoza is quite literally kicked out. Altofronto and Maria reassume power, loyal followers are rewarded, but Maquerelle is dismissed to the suburbs, and Bilioso is merely let live: "You to my worst frend I would hardly give:/ Thou art a perfect olde knave" (1. 215). In the same manner, Lafew takes up Parolles at the end of *All's Well That Ends Well*. But, finally, it is the metaphor of the actor that is heard as Altofronto looks at his court: "The rest of idle actors idly part" (1. 215).

III   *Altofronto Disguised as Malevole*

The most notable of the actors who part at the end of *The Malcontent* is, of course, Malevole. He appears to vanish as soon as he unmasks and the gathered court hails him as "Duke Altofront," and the cornets flourish jubilantly. But the mark he makes upon the play, upon the spectators, and upon Altofronto, cannot be so simply set aside. As Altofronto, he is the temporizer, the embodiment of sensible stoicism; as Malevole, he is the spitting critic and the energetic revenger; he is both a member of society and a scathing commentator on it. As the hero of a revenge comedy, he is both judge and revenger: a detached observer, he works within the law; the directly engaged prosecutor, he bends the law when he is not placing himself outside it altogether. His impersonal view of society has to accommodate itself to his personal quarrel with society. His double purpose is to win back his Dukedom and to cleanse society. One is never quite sure which purpose has precedence or whether indeed the two can be so nicely separated.

The conflict between admiration and distaste cannot be simply resolved by admiring Altofronto and disliking Malevole. The conflict in one man's character between righteous anger and rancor, powerful scorn and cheap cynicism, sobriety and wildness, necessary harshness and a "hydeous imagination," is marvelously sharpened by the device of Altofronto and by the disguise he assumes; but the conflict is blurred from time to time because of lack of clarity as to how much he is of the world that he inveighs against and how much he is outside it. From this duality emerge both the forceful clarities and the tantalizing ambiguities of the play.

Altofronto, whatever the passion burning within him that enables him to sustain the character of Malevole so energetically, is fundamentally a sober, wise, careful man. His wisdom and sobriety lead him to take positions that are disturbingly sensitive to the intricacies of realpolitik as well as deeply perceptive of man's being capable of reason rather than his being ruled by reason. As Malevole, his angry melancholy at the state of the world and man's self-destructive brutishness at times take him almost beyond rule by reason. And yet, paradoxically, he is most anguished by the sight of virtue—Maria's in prison—and his mask slips; he speaks momentarily as Altofronto, detesting the role he has to play. Then with an immense self-control, he pulls himself together and observes that he "better play the foole Lord, then be the foole Lord" (1.204).

In a court of fools ranging from the vacuous to the dangerous, his choice of the role of bitter fool is shrewd. Bravado is foolishness, and the hectic career of Mendoza proves it. Altofronto soberly chooses to play the part of a wildman: it is a part that is unsuitable for such a man, and yet he has the motive and the cue for passion. It is, indeed, his very qualities that make his transformation into Malevole not only brilliant but dangerous—his "prodigious affections" (1.146) are sometimes so convincing that it is hard to accept them as pretense. Marston, as we have seen, was interested in the prodigious, in exaggeration, in testing a genre—or a role—to its limits, and beyond them. As a play, *The Malcontent* is "essentially visual . . . [it] insist[s] on being played and watched" as it self-consciously exploits its theatricalism.[4] Altofronto also (self-consciously ?) chose to play a role that allowed him to express his justifiable anger at society with a free, and sometimes uncontrolled, spirit. But he is playing the role of Malevole, he is not—or ought not to be—Malevole. In other plays, Marston directly discussed the actor's art and his relationship with his role, but in *The Malcontent,* this interest is an implicit part of the play. If theatricalism is the mainspring of the play, it is nowhere more obvious than in the acting and impersonation that happens within the action. Altofronto, Pietro, and Mendoza are all actors; and, in the final masque, Ferneze and Celso can be added to the roster. The stage direction telling the reader that Malevole shifts his speech is a direct reminder to the reader of what the man in the theater can see and hear for himself—that Malevole is an impersonation by Altofronto.

The effect of an impersonation usually rests in exaggeration of the basic traits of the person or type copied. The reaction to a superb impersonation is that of admiration, but also of awareness of an impersonation. Marston, recognizing this fact, cleverly tries to discount it by unleashing the full force of Malevole's malcontentedness on an unprepared audience, which takes it for what it is. Only when the ruse is revealed to it can the normal reaction to an impersonation begin to work.

In the theater, the abrasive vigor of Malevole can appear as a facet of a characteristic performance. The denunciation can run freely and forcefully, but the dangers of its being overdone are held in check—to a certain extent at least—for both the actor and the audience by the fact of the impersonation. This awareness, of course, does not mean that Malevole is taken for granted in any casual way by the audience; he is not made colorless, uncertain, or merely vaguely hopeful: he acts with dispatch when the occasion demands; and, amid the confusion and strife at court, his coolness is impressive. He shows that it craves not only wit to play the fool, but courage to play the waiting game and to let everyone else get caught in the action which he is pleased to control. As a revenger, Malevole is conventional in biding his time; but few revengers delay for such calculated reasons as he does. These qualities are as necessary to him as Altofronto as they are to him as Malevole.

IV *Marston as Malevole*

The actor's burden is to portray a man who is brilliantly imitating someone else. The fundamental difficulty, however, resides in the question of how to play Altofronto. The malcontentedness of Malevole is relatively straightforward; he is a "humour" character, but Altofronto is not. Altofronto acts the part so well that it appears natural to him; it is not all impersonation. The same confusion is sensed between Marston the author and Marston in the role of the Satyre in *The Scourge of Villanie*. Possibly a neat distinction between the two aspects of Malevole and of Marston cannot be made, and Marston wins in *The Malcontent* the plaudits he does because he has managed to dramatize so effectively a fundamental duality in his own character.

Instead of thrusting himself and his opinions with varying success into the play, he writes a play about just such a character as himself. Marston, the serious young man concerned about the depravity of the world and about man's betrayal of himself, and Marston, the wild young man who plays the role of the Satyre with a suspicious relish, are the dual personality reflected in Altofronto-Malevole. He dramatizes, in both the good and bad senses of the word, his own situation as a serious man driven into taking the part of a railing wildman, with all the risks entailed, in order to shock a largely unheeding and corrupt society into awareness. It would be foolish, however, to press this comparison too far; Marston is not writing an autobiographical play. Nonetheless, some of the play's strengths as a dramatic satire may owe a debt to the similarity between the essential situation *The Malcontent* portrays and the position in which Marston found himself in his own time, as least as far as he saw it.

V *Morality and* The Malcontent

Superficially, all works neatly and smoothly for Altofronto's benefit. He manages affairs very skillfully. Villainy, craftily encouraged, overreaches itself and destroys itself; the usurper repents his evil action; and Altofronto returns to power. Marston, however, offers no panaceas and does not close with visions of cosy happiness. The ills of society are not cured, but they have been ruthlessly diagnosed. Many of its members have been stripped of unthinking acceptance of what Marston would call "Opinion," and then are hopefully made better. Among them is Altofronto himself. During the course of the action, he undergoes a trial and a strengthening through pain as he comes to realize the virulence of the social disease in his land. As Duke, he had been weak and culpable to some extent in allowing affairs to fall to such a miserable condition. Realization of this fact shocks and concerns him and is made more painful as he appreciates the price he has unknowingly demanded of the few decent people in his court—the faithful Celso, the loyal captain of the Citadel, and, above all, his patiently enduring and loving wife. Altofronto castigates the world for its general decay as well as for the particular ill fortune he had visited upon himself. The survival of the qualities of loyalty and affection in his friends; his own common sense and his maturity, which does not preclude a fierce anger at the corruption about him; and his molding of his satiric criticism to fit an adopted role that demands extremity of view, combine to give an unusual depth to his commentary.

Malevole's reaction to the corruption of the Genoese court brings the play closest to the traditional morality play. Broad resemblances to the morality play are obvious—Mendoza is the Corrupt Man who destroys himself, whereas Pietro is the Good Man who falters and is then restored to uprightness. Pietro's restoration is an especially hard-won one because Malevole, who is remorseless with him, insists that he hold the mirror not only before his wife and the court but before himself. It may not be using too strong a term to suggest that Pietro finds "salvation" by recognizing his own weakness, by forgiving his wife, and by restoring the dukedom to Altofronto. Pietro and Aurelia, at the end of the play, retire to a life of contemplation. The court is called a Hell, and the final reconciliations are formally

attributed to Providence. In act 3, Pietro, wondering at the irony of a
situation that drives him to find proof of his wife's dishonor, says:

> good God, that men should
> Desire to search out that, which being found kils all
> Their joye of life: to taste the tree of Knowledge,
> And then be driven out of Paradice.
>
> (1.174)

This statement does not make the play a Christian allegory; for as
G. K. Hunter observes, "The Elizabethan stage was a *secular* stage, in
the sense that it did not meddle with specifically religious subjects;
but, on the other hand, both the authors and the audiences were
deeply involved with religious assumptions and emotions throughout
their ordinary lives, and it would be very odd if these did not seep
through into their handling of ostensibly secular, but serious and
deeply felt, situations."[5] Religion was always a serious matter for
Marston; and, however far he was on the road to priesthood when he
wrote this play, he did not use religious imagery carelessly.

Marston's use of the morality play outline does not mean a
presentation of clear-cut problems and simple confrontations. When
the morality play is observed in Marston, it takes on that curious
property of reflections, a subtle reversal. For all the boldness of
Marston's colors, he does not work in plain blacks and whites. Pietro
is far more than merely a Good Man who falters because the world in
which he lives is more dangerous and sophisticated than the
old-fashioned world of the morality play. His words as he leads the
guards to Aurelia's bedroom are more than merely conventional:

> I strike but yet like him that gainst stone walles
> Directs his shafts, reboundes in his owne face,
> My Ladies shame is mine, O God tis mine.
> . . . . O Gentlemen
> God knowes I love her, nothing els, but this,
> I am not well . . . .
> I have no childe, all that my youth begot,
> Hath bin your loves.
>
> (1.166–67)

This moving and direct expression of sympathetic human feeling is
rare in the play. Pietro trusts the wrong man; his wife is the
conventional, brazen adulteress; but these misfortunes only sharpen

the poignancy of his feeling. He does not relish his task nor its fulfillment; and, in his anguish, he, like other Marstonian men, spurns the comforts of Senecan precepts: "Out upon him, he writ of Temperance and Fortitude, yet lived like a voluptuous Epicure, and died like an effeminate coward" (1.174). Pietro is here the "Good Man" of sensitivity as well as the unusual avenger who goes without fury about his vengeance and finds no reward in it. He is brought more convincingly to repentance than many characters in Elizabethan drama—Aurelia's change of heart is a good example of the more typical instant conversion—but, thereafter, the demands of the plot allow Pietro to be little more than an effective partner for Malevole.

The figure of the Vice is also used in some unexpected ways. Malevole steps forward in an old-time manner; but, instead of revealing further and deeper villainy, he announces beliefs and plans that prove him a man bent on righting wrongs: he is vice turned inside out. This reversal balances well with Mendoza who soliloquizes in a more traditional style only after his first soliloquy had suggested, against expectation perhaps, that he was a court amorist rather than a Machiavellian. The modes of revenge tragedy are essentially used, as are those of the morality play, to sharpen the impact of comedy. Marston has learned how to adopt and to adapt a device so that the two ways he uses work toward an exciting unity.

VI *The Contrivances of Revenge Comedy*

The revenges of *The Malcontent* are as odd as the revengers. Altofronto seeks revenge, not of blood, but of the heart's awareness on Pietro. The latter learns to abandon cries of "Revenge" and to have a more philosophical and Christian view. He himself, who ought to be pursued to his doom by Altofronto, is instead hounded to his salvation. Mendoza has all the attributes of the villainous revenger save that he is unable to kill anyone. He takes up his stance as a revenger while he is the lover of the Duke's wife; he is pursuing not the Duke but another of the Duchess's lovers.

Because of Altofronto's revenge decisions, the regular formulas of revenge tragedy do not produce the usual results. Since he controls the action, the intriguers are doomed to failure, murder is prevented, and villainous plots bring confusion and self-defeat to the plotters. This control minimizes the acts of the villains, but it does not reduce the villains to a farcical procession of freaks. Mendoza, for instance, is a powerful force for evil, the single person who can hold his own with Altofronto. His continual planning, cleverly ruthless though it is, fails because of his reliance upon the wrong man and because he himself does so little and that carelessly. Nevertheless, he is never allowed to degenerate into the mustachioed villain of melodrama. He is a Machiavellian who is undermined without being made to appear as merely cheaply ludicrous; and, as a result, he engenders the same mixture of laughter and unease as a Herod. A mark of his stature is that many feel his punishment should be more severe than it is.

Mendoza is never the commanding figure that he himself thinks he is. His first appearance, albeit momentary, as a foolish lover who is deceived, leaves an impression that is never quite erased. His craftiness is undeniable but is always exercised under Malevole's control. The dark shadows of the court are real; the courtiers are more foolish than vicious; but their activity takes on darker color because of Malevole's presence among them and because of the serious lessons Pietro learns in their court. Mendoza always tries to resolve his problems by killing; but, in comedy, death is not a resolver of issues. Dark though the world of *The Malcontent* is, the successful issue of events has been carefully signaled. Because Mendoza insists upon acting like the revengeful villain of tragedy in what is a comedy, he is ultimately reduced to laughable proportions. Even at his most savage, he is as ineffectual as when he failed to kill Ferneze. As a would-be master criminal and as an absolute dictator, he is fittingly dismissed by being kicked out, like the petty criminal that he is, by Altofronto.

Complexity of contrivance is a feature of comedy, and in *The Malcontent* the action takes on more the air of bustling intrigue than of purposeful movement to inescapable evil. Throughout the play, a discrepancy appears between what is planned and what happens. Altofronto's mistake originally had been to sleep "in fearlesse vertue, Suspectles, too suspectles" (1.151). Mendoza's mistake is to go to the other extreme by suspecting everyone and by plotting endlessly. The better way is not to expect either a perfectly good or a totally evil world, but to recognize this one for what it is and to work sensibly and hopefully for good. In this play, the worthwhile people come to know goodness, even to be good, not to be perfect. By this token, Mendoza is a small-minded man who is punished for his achievement as a bad troublemaker rather than for the larger crimes he failed to perpetrate.

Mendoza is dealt with summarily, almost as briefly as his kinsman

Don John in *Much Ado About Nothing*. Comedy traditionally takes the lighter-hearted line that merrily promotes the uniting of happy young people in marriage by means of the amusing circumvention of obstacles and the thwarting of sharp tricksters by sharper and wittier tricksters or by the accidents of bumblers. Marston's comedy deals with mature people (youth is a stuff that has not endured in Genoa), and he brings about more earnest conclusions. Most comedies end in happy marriages made between young men and women; Marston reunites couples already married: their marriages are reaffirmed after separations caused by imprisonment or by adultery repented. As romantic ardor is eschewed, so are prankish jolly intrigues and obstacles: matters of plot are sterner, and Malevole and Mendoza are scarcely to be labeled as "tricksters" in a cheerful comic world.

The Malcontent uses traditions of romantic comedy only to deny them. A jaundiced eye strips the Illyrian scene of warmth and amiability. There is indeed a world of difference between Sir Andrew Aguecheek buying Sir Toby Belch's aid in his love affair and Ferneze's purchase of Maquerelle's aid in his pursuit of Aurelia. In Genoa, love exists but too often degrades to lust. The comedy of Feste becomes the harsh wit of Malevole, and Malvolio's self-love darkens to a rasher and more dangerous expression in Mendoza. Marston's is, of course, a darker comedy; and the meeting between his somewhat uncongenial material and the comic method produces some of the most tantalizing reverberations in the play.

The Malcontent is Marston's image of the unexpectedness and of the imbalance of everyday life; of the way familiar things, when they are seen in odd lights or occur in unforeseen patterns, are at once grotesque and yet just sufficiently ordinary to be disconcerting. The vision of the satires and of *The Historie of Antonio and Mellida* is presented more clearly and with greater artistic maturity in *The Malcontent*. Marston was to test this vision in other ways, but he wrote nothing that was conspicuously better than *The Malcontent*.

CHAPTER 7

The Dutch Curtezan

IN the Prologue to *The Dutch Curtezan*, Marston suavely equivo-
cates about delight and instruction. On the one hand, he promises
to present, in what he calls, "this easie Play," not "what you would,
but what we may." His pen may "seeme over slight," but that is
because he aims to delight rather than to instruct. On the other hand,
he adjures the same audience: "Thinke and then speake: tis
rashnesse, and not wit/ To speake what is in passion, and not
judgement fit." And, bearing in mind his reputation for satiric furor,
he adds: "Yet thinke not, but like others raile we could,/ (Best art
Presents, not what it can, but should)." In this play he intends to offer
precepts in a wiser way. His pen will only "seeme" slight because he
does not now strive, as he once vociferously did, to instruct; he has
learned the rashness of speaking out of uninhibited passion. The play,
indeed, is to develop this very theme in the character of Malheureux,
the unusual protagonist that Marston proposes:

> Nothing but passionate man in his slight play,
> Who hath this onely ill: to some deem'd worst,
> A modest diffidence, and selfe mistrust.
>
> (2.69)

An "easie Play," a "slight play," it nonetheless asks of its audience
careful judgment; and in this respect, it is a Marstonian play.

The plot material that he announces certainly sounds straightforward: "The difference betwixt the love of a Curtezan, & a wife, is the
full scope of the Play, which intermixed with the deceits of a wittie
Citie Jester, fils up the Comedie" (2.69). But this statement is also
blandly deceptive. The subject announced is ordinary material for a
comedy in another writer's hands, but Marston does not take
questions of love, lust, and marriage lightly. *The Dutch Curtezan*

contains Marston's most exuberant comedy, but it can nevertheless justifiably be called "the fullest and frankest as well as the most subtle and perceptive study of sexual psychology to be found anywhere in the drama of [Marston's] period."[1] Moreover, for his audience, the "Characters, incidents and language had to meet very definite expectations. While the audience demanded novelty in the bill, they wanted conformity to the pattern."[2] As a professional playwright (and company shareholder), Marston knew the force of what the audience would like; and his skill was in his fulfillment of the mild "but what we may" present (2.69).

In this play, Francischina is the courtesan whose love Freevill gives up for that of Beatrice, his wife-to-be. Freevill insists on making a final visit to Francischina despite the protests of his friend, Malheureux, a priggish, inexperienced man who puts his trust in a cloistered virtue. Reluctantly, he agrees to go to see the courtesan with Freevill: "Ile go to make her loath the shame shee's in. The sight of vice augments the hate of sinne" (2.75). The sight of Francischina, however, rouses only infatuation in Malheureux; and his turmoil is increased when she makes Freevill's death the price of her favors. When Malheureux reveals the plight he is in to Freevill, the latter realizes that a shock will be needed to bring his friend back to his senses; for Malheureux, who still recognizes the strength of his moral scruples, cannot abandon his friendship for Freevill and yet must possess Franchischina.

The two men fake a quarrel, and Freevill hides so that Malheureux can tell Francischina that he has satisfied her demand and killed his friend. When he goes to her, she betrays him to the law; and Freevill also seems to have betrayed him and cannot be found. Malheureux's protestations that the whole thing was a hoax are dismissed, and he is condemned to death. Only at the scaffold does Freevill reappear and save his now enlightened friend. As excuse for the anguish that his disappearance had caused, Freevill claims that "a friend / Should waigh no action, but the actions end" (2.134). This claim Shakespeare's Helena made to Diana and the widow in *All's Well That Ends Well:* "All's well that ends well, still the fines the Crowne: / What ere the course, the end is the renowne" (4.2479–80).

Marston's tolerant treatment of his material can still exacerbate. "It reflects a popular audience of early Jacobean days and offers crude entertainment for crude minds."[3] The central situation turns on an old joke—a "good" man in "love" with a cheap woman; the Puritan infatuated with "the most odious spectacle the earth can present . . .

an immodest vulger woman" (2.75); "The man of dignity is driven to undignified lengths."[4] Marston is predictably awkward because he insists on exploring the joke: "lets neere be ashamd to speake what we be not ashamed to think, I dare as boldly speake venery, as think venery . . . for my owne part I consider nature without apparell, without disguising of custome or complement, I give thoughts wordes, and wordes truth, and truth boldnes" (2.98–99).

Marston takes this declaration from Montaigne, but the argument and its handling are his own. Boldness is not made an excuse for tedious dirt; speech is free but not unrestrained. Marston's broad, frank, and sometimes vulgar treatment raises laughter, not sniggers; he offers boisterous jests, not smut. The same morass that he viewed in the verse satires he sees now with an eye no longer glazed by the intensity of his gaze; for, unlike the author of *Pigmalion's Image*, Marston can now distinguish between love and lust in no banal way. The moral view he espouses may be dismissed as "conventional," but to do so not only treats morality more casually than Marston does, but also ignores both his view and the arguments with which he supports it.

Freevill learned to distinguish between the two kinds of love: "I lov'd her [Francischina] with my heart, untill my soule shewed me the imperfection of my body, and placed my affection on a lawfull love, my modest *Beatrice*" (2.78). Malheureux, who knows nothing of either lust or love, can only recoil at Freevill's admitting having enjoyed the pleasures of the town and his gaily insisting that they were pleasures. The basic situation is a common one: essentially, it is the morality play plot of youthful ignorance—the simple Lusty Juvenutus—narrowly saved from sin. Malheureux, however, is far more sophisticated than such a young hero, and Marston's play is richer and subtler than its prototype. Cyrus Hoy has perceptively commented that Malheureux "is agonizingly aware of what he is, or what he ought to be, and what he is in process of becoming. Throughout most of the play, Marston keeps him impaled tormentingly on the horns of the familiar dilemma and, his self-consciousness being what it is, he can never for a moment close his eyes to the incongruity of his posture. He recognizes his shame; he defines it explicitly, and the effect is laughable, touching and, for him, excruciating. The anomaly of his position is never lost on him, a fact which compounds the irony of his plight."[5]

This situation allows Marston to let his comedy range from wit to farce while never quite losing a sense of the complexities caused by trying to balance what the Prologue called "passion" and "judgement"—that the problem posed to those caught in the "familiar dilemma" cannot be resolved either by simply suspending judgment or by exercising an absolute moral rigor. Man's plans must be suited to man's capacities for he is, after all, only *animal rationis capax*, an animal capable of reason.

I *The Double Plot*

The wide-ranging comedy of *The Dutch Curtezan* is filled up (as Marston modestly puts it) with a brilliantly developed subplot that exhibits the "deceits of a wittie Citie Jester," called Cocledemoy, as they are practiced on the luckless vintner, Mulligrub. Cocledemoy is also a drinking acquaintance of Freevill, and, before the play begins, he has made off from Mulligrub's tavern with some cups. He had disguised himself as a barber; and, while Mulligrub was lathered blind, he had left with the money set out to replace the cups. Later Mulligrub buys a bowl from Burnish, a goldsmith, and has it sent to his tavern. There Cocledemoy passes himself off as Burnish's man with a salmon, tells Mrs. Mulligrub to prepare dinner for the Burnishes who are coming back with her husband, and takes away the bowl to have some arms graven on it. Mulligrub begins the salmon, finds out that the bowl has gone, and runs off to Burnish's. This is Cocledemoy's cue. He reappears, saying it was all a joke and everyone is to eat at Burnish's house. He goes on ahead with the remains of the salmon. Finally, when pursued by Mulligrub, Cocledemoy drops his cloak, reports it stolen, and has Mulligrub arrested as a thief when the latter runs in with the cloak he picked up in the chase as a clue to the thief. Once again, only on the day of execution does Cocledemoy uncover and, having won Mulligrub's forgiveness, return all the stolen properties.

A third episode, too slight to be called a plot, that is run with the main story, demonstrates the wit of Crispinella, Beatrice's sister; her wooing by Tysefew, "a blunt Gallant"; and the discomfiture of Caqueteur, "a pratling Gull."

The fullest scope of the play embraces the differences between one woman's love and another's, between one wife's love and another's. In a play concerned with marriage, the humdrum one of the Mulligrubs passes oblique comment on the institution. Mrs. Mulligrub's arrangements to assuage her widowhood even when her husband is on the way to the gallows cannot bear weighty interpretation, but they are a neat comment about one kind of fidelity—to enjoyment of sex. Perhaps Marston was remembering how Chaucer's Wife of Bath "folwed ay myn inclinacioun" and gave her heart to "Jankin oure clerk" as her fifth husband while they followed the coffin of her fourth husband. The prosaic love of the Mulligrubs can be contrasted with the other kinds of love of the characters in the play: the romantic in Freevill and Beatrice, the casual in Cocledemoy and Mary Faugh, the twisted in Francischina's for Freevill, and the brusquely witty in that of Tysefew and Crispinella.

Both plots are intricate and give pleasure in their nimble twists and turns. On the surface, they appear to be as different as those of separate plays, but they do make one play. They are harnessed to run in the same direction; and, if they are not always in step, the syncopations all work to the same comic end. The subplot revolves around themes and situations that farcically reflect those of the main plot. The main plot turns on a trick intended to open a man's eyes to the world; the subplot, on tricks that are used more to baffle Mulligrub than to clarify matters for him. Freevill jests for a purpose; Cocledemoy, for jesting's sake. The main plot uses the devices of melodrama and romance; the subplot abuses them. All of this sharing of material allows glancing allusions, passing resemblances, balancing of situations, that tend to unite satisfyingly the different actions.

II   *The Mingling of Delight and Instruction*

Marston controls the comic atmosphere of *The Dutch Curtezan* with great skill; it is a comedy about a problem, not a problem comedy. Although his major themes receive serious comment, they are never made the excuse for solemnity. Malheureux is too pompous to be tragic; what he says is not always foolish, but his is essentially a ludicrous position. Moreover, his temptress is a caricature of a villainess; that he takes her so seriously when all others see her for what she is, heightens his folly. Likewise, Freevill is intelligent, quick-witted, and sensible rather than noble or heroic. Marston looks at his characters with neither the intensity of the satirist nor with the indulgence of a sentimentalist. The skill with which he sets his mood, states his theme, and pursues his argument is well shown in the opening scenes.

After the young men have chaffed the miserable Mulligrub in these opening scenes about his losses at the hands of Cocledemoy, Malheureux and Freevill begin to argue about morality. Malheureux's position is one familiar in Marston:

> Know Sir, the strongest argument that speakes
> Against the soules eternitie is lust,
> That Wisemans folly, and the fooles wisedome.
>
> (2.73)

Malheureux plays the wiseman, but his strong arguments are vitiated because they are rooted in ignorance and are propounded with cold narrow-mindedness. Nonetheless, lust is to be his folly. He reckons Freevill the fool; but Freevill has learned wisdom—the value of true love; and so he can safely play the fool when he counters Malherueux's arguments with a witty parody of a legal-defense speech on the behalf of brothels. The peroration in this speech rises briefly and powerfully from parody to fierce irony before it closes in a tongue-in-cheek manner:

> They sell their bodies: doe not better persons sell their
> soules? nay, since all things have been sould, honor, justice,
> faith: nay, even God himselfe:
> Aye me, what base ignoblenesse is it,
> To sell the pleasure of a wanton bed?
> . . . .
> For this I hold to be deny'd of no man,
> All thinges are made for man, and man for woman,
> Give me my fee!
>
> (2.74)

His fee, as it were, is Malheureux's agreement to go with him "to a house! of salvation." "Salvation?" asks Malheureux. "Yes," replies Freevill, more wisely than he knows perhaps, " 'twill make thee repent" (2.75).

They leave, and Cocledemoy enters with Mary Faugh, a plain, nondescript creature whom he genially refers to as a "necessary damnation"—one among a host of insults he sends her way in the swagger of casual affection. He delivers a blunt appraisal of the bawd and her profession. He prefers to see clearly, if kindly, whether, bawds are as plain as Mary Faugh or as undeniably attractive as Francischina. Malheureux is quite unable to make such a judgment; for, as he enters, Mary is the first sight of vice that he has had after his solemn moralizing; she is so drab that he never notices her; and she is sent to fetch Francischina. Cocledemoy leaves the two young men to ponder the ordinariness and inescapability of love: "a wise man, when hee is in his belly act, lookes like a foole" (2.77). This comment chimes significantly with Malheureux's lofty comment about wisemen and fools.

When Francischina arrives, Malheureux does indeed gaze on her silently, "like a foole." Freevill and Cocledemoy have given ample warning about the deceitful appeal of the beautiful bawd—her own heavy accent, and her outrageously equivocal song—but these now count for nothing to Malherureux. He doggedly argues with himself about the rightness of his passionate feeling, but he turns his arguments on himself and claims the last word: "Of all the fooles that would all man out-thrust, / He that 'gainst Nature would seeme wise is worst" (2.80). Malheureux tries to justify his change of heart by asserting that "no love's without some lust, no life without some love" (2.80), and the meaning of this assertion is probed not only in his reactions but in those of Beatrice and Freevill, and of Crispinella and Tysefew. In the verse satires, women had borne much of the blame for the world's obsession with lust; in this play, the maturer view is convincingly argued.

III   Stock Characters Freshly Handled

Francischina is a traditional figure: she is the wicked fairy whose plots must fail. A cheap, scheming harlot whose beauty is undermined by her grotesque accent (the English, rich in their own dialects, always find foreigners' English endlessly funny), her cunning works in a comic environment in which all her plans must fail. In some ways, she is an inventive reworking of Mendoza. Her actions spring from bitterness and jealousy; and, like Malheureux, she takes herself too seriously. Such comparisons can be made because she is not a cardboard villainess; she is "drawn with Dutch fidelity; she is displayed without exposition as a savage, murderous, treacherous beauty, whose sweetness of appearance, and whose dancing and songs are shown making their full effect upon a man who despises her but cannot free himself from her enchantment. She is the Dark Lady of the Comedies."[6]

Beatrice also is a stock character—the faithful, pure heroine who is almost doomed to be pale and uninteresting. Marston makes her constancy natural and acceptable because of her simple definitions of love and her unaffected living by them: she loves and asks nothing in return. She loves Freevill, and she cannot alter because he seems not to love her. Similarly, she cannot hate Francischina merely because Freevill once loved her. The unrequited lover can usually claim little real sympathy, for he demands to be loved merely because he himself loves. Beatrice, the opposite of this tedious type of lover, believes that love casts out fear, understands all, and forgives all. This Christian love is not expanded at length, but it is a development of the conventional and sweet acceptance of ill-fortune expected of romantic heroines. The conventional romantic heroine does not, however, speak with Beatrice's quiet rightness: "He did not ill not to love me, but sure hee did not well to mocke me: Gentle mindes will pittie, though they cannot love: yet peace, and my love sleepe with him" (2.119). The most direct statement of the difference between the love of a wife and that of the courtesan is found in the difference expressed here between Beatrice and the gloating Francischina.

Marston places Beatrice and her feelings so accurately and so strongly that her love for Freevill and his for her need no grand rhapsodic affirmation. In their one important scene together in act 2, Freevill and Beatrice demonstrate their love in strong rather than in passionate language. The tart wooing that Marston could manage so well he gives to Crispinella and Tysefew. The variety they bring is needed to make the case that, just as there are different kinds of courtesan, there are also different kinds of wife.

Crispinella, for all her brusque talk, is clearly a decent, honorable girl. She speaks directly but never disgustingly; she can be broad but is never obscene. She and Tysefew are always a likable couple who are tilting at each other and who are not a pair of ranting vulgarians. They are a rough version of Beatrice and Benedick, and the roughness is capably defended by Crispinella: "she whose honest freenes makes it her vertue, to speake what she thinks, will make it her necessity to thinke what is good, I love no prohibited things, and yet I would have nothing prohibited by policy but by vertue" (2.99). She speaks in commonsense terms about the kind of things that Cocledemoy acts out in farcical outrageousness. There are obvious indications of the Restoration heroine in Crispinella, and even of Shavian women; in her own time, she makes a welcome change from the slyer frankness

and salacity of Fletcherian Jacobean ladies-in-waiting. She and
Tysefew are good examples of the realistic treatment that Marston
often intends; they are good-humored exempla of themes generally
more sharply and fiercely treated.

Mrs. Mulligrub is a fine, smug hypocrite whose hypocrisy, unlike
that of Malheureux, which is forgivable and curable, is mean and
ignorant. She is a snobbish wife who is frantically trying to climb the
social ladder and who is financing her climb by watering the beer and
by falsifying the accounts. She is gullible only in the cause of social
snobbery, she is well matched with Mulligrub, and their marriage is
seen through a farcical glass.

IV The Technical Skills of an "Easie Play"

The women and their men are not set against each other in
mechanical patterns of mathematical precision, but they illustrate the
central argument in their actions. Familiar themes from the verse
satires appear in the play. Sometimes, as in Caqueteur, the mincing
fop lives to display his clothes and jewels; and, though the action
would not stumble without him, he decorates it amusingly. Elsewhere, the method of glancing reference, carelessly yet cleverly
scattered, accumulating unobtrusively to resonate in the mind, is
well handled. The debasement of religion is treated in this fashion.
The smooth coin of accepted religious reference is passed so glibly by
some, that one knows their piety is only an empty show, as hollow as
their oaths and cries. Marston has no sermon to preach; and he sets up
an example in Beatrice whose religion is more than conventional
piety, but he properly lets this seriousness remain in the background
to be lit by incidental flashes from others.

At the very start, Mulligrub is mockingly told by the young men to
repent his sins of the cellar; and this jesting is followed by
Malheureux's taking his unpleasant stand on a narrow piety. Even
Mary Faugh can mock his earnest avowal with her unexpected
religious claim: "call a woman the most ungodly names: I must
confess we all eate of the forbidden fruite, and for mine owne part
tho I am one of the family of love and as they say a bawd that covers the
multitude of sinnes, yet I trust I am none of the wicked that eate fish a
Fridaies" (2.76). Mrs. Mulligrub, who is particularly fond of her
religious feelings, regularly polishes them in pious reference. She
neatly combines religion with the rise of her capitalism in her

endeavors to recoup losses: "Good husband take comfort in the Lord, Ile play the Divell, but ile recover it, have a good conscience. 'Tis but a weekes cutting in the Terme" (2.97).

These are the qualities of Marston's best art and are visible throughout the play. The music, for instance, is always both a pleasing entertainment and an integral part of the action. Francischina sings her song very naturally, and its lilt sets off the pleasure that Freevill takes in it as well as Malheureux's stunned reception of it. He is probably the only person, onstage and off, who hears it as a charmingly sung love song rather than as a prostitute's musical advertisement. Its double purpose and Malheureux's unawareness of it add to the pleasure the song gives. The wedding of Freevill and Beatrice demands a masqued dance, and the plot uses it neatly as the bright setting for the sudden fake quarrel between Freevill and Malheureux. Poor Mulligrub ends a couple of acts despairingly by calling for music to soothe his tortured breast; and, although tavern-keepers always called for the fiddlers to play for their customers, Mulligrub amusingly calls them for himself. The result is an extra delight because Marston makes his inter-act music a part of his play.

Examples have been indicated of Marston's setting the people and their speeches in the first act in small patterns within the large design of the act. The sight of plain Mary Faugh does not augment Malheureux's hate of sin, but Francischina's beauty transforms it. Freevill's mock defense of brothels is matched by Cocledemoy's equally scintillating but more straightforward disquisition about bawds. This correlation is carried forward throughout the action. In act 4, the mock quarrel at the masque is followed by the crisp wooing of Tysefew and Crispinella, which sounds quite as combative but whose real intent is affection. At the end of act 4, the night is the setting for the betrayal of Malheureux to the law and for Cocledemoy's antics in the case of the purloined cloak, which sees Mulligrub similarly betrayed.

Perhaps the greatest art of *The Dutch Curtezan* is the comic balance that Marston maintains through its course. No one character runs away with the play, not even Cocledemoy; and nothing is painted in simple black and white. Possibly some of Marston's own experience is in his depiction of Malheureux, who speaks like the young Marston, if not in his hectoring tone at least with his superiority. Moreover, Malheureux has to learn Marston's lesson—

that the sight of vice is as likely to be dangerously attractive as morally
forbidding. Malheureux, who is oddly perceptive about himself at
times, recognizes his own awkwardness:

> I shall neere proove hartely receaved,
> A kinde of flat ungratious modesty,
> An insufficient dulnes staines my haviour.

(2.84)

These moments humanize him and mark the pleasantness that lies
hidden in his priggishness. Something of the same feeling emerges in
his struggles with his feelings. If he does have any connection with
the earlier Marston, he is delineated with some subtlety by the
maturer man. Like the best of Marston's characterization, he is not a
simple cardboard figure.

The play leads by a complicated path, amid much laughter, to the
making of a man wiser about friendship, love, and vice. *All's Well
That Ends Well* touches upon some of the same issues, and Bertram
and Malheureux have to learn the same lesson. Helena and Freevill
both go to dangerous lengths, which they insist must be allowed, to
teach that lesson. Helena evokes so much sympathy and Bertram so
little that the balance of her play is hardly maintained.[7] Marston avoids
that kind of serious sympathy which is so hard to contain within a
satirical comedy, or in any comedy that depends upon contrivance
and ancient tricks to arrive at a desired conclusion. Possibly
Marston's conclusion is not more successful than Shakespeare's, for
Marston relinquishes some of the moral drive of his comedy as he
unravels all his plots in a brilliant concerted finale. Marston's comedy
and Shakespeare's might best be compared insofar as they approach a
similar theme in different ways, and both prove the riskiness of their
ventures.

Marston brings home valuable rewards from his venture. The last
word in his play, the last displays, are Cocledemoy's; but the last and
quieter words are Malheureux's, and with them the main plot is
rounded out. They apply to his role in the play, and they also apply to
Marston's own condition and learning after his progress from the
raucous verse satires to this ebullient play that is so well compacted
with instruction and delight:

> I am myselfe, how long wast ere I could
> Perswade my passion to grow calme to you?
> Rich sence makes good bad language, and a friend

> Should waigh no action, but the actions end.
> I am now worthie yours, when before
> The beast of man, loose bloud distemperd us,
> "He that lust rules cannot be vertuous."

(2.134)

As Malheureux's, the sentiments are little changed from those that he had expressed at the start of the play; as Marston's, they are little different from what he professed at the start of his writing career. Nonetheless, both men have won from experience a better understanding of them and a solid right to assert them.

CHAPTER 8

Parasitaster, or The Fawne

THE Inns of Court celebrated Christmas long and heartily. At the Middle Temple, where Marston lived for upwards of ten years, the festivities were ruled over by a Prince D'Amour; and they included feasts, dancing, games, mock trials, and other legal jollity, as well as masques and plays. Traditionally, such features as the mock trials, debates, and special speeches were repeated from year to year. Recently, the influence of these festivities on Marston's plays has been assessed by Philip Finkelpearl, who suggests that *Histriomastix* was intended for the Christmas revels of 1598–99 and that *The Fawne*, if it was not performed at a later Christmas celebration, uses material that was a staple of the Middle Temple revelry at that time.[1]

The Prince D'Amour naturally concerned himself with love; and mock trials of types of lovers and amusing speeches on topics such as women's inconstancy were regular features of the entertainment. The notion of a Court of Love is an old one, but, whether Marston knew of it from his reading, in using the device in *The Fawne*, he was probably benefiting from direct acquaintance in his own Inn. Other details in the play may refer to life in the Inns, for the matter of the laundress's letter being passed off by a foolish would-be lover as an aristocratic lady's love letter has its topicality. Laundresses were the only women allowed in the students' rooms in the Inns, and the results were predictable ones according to legend and jest. Since an air of fun at lawyers' expense hovers over *The Fawne*, Finkelpearl has concluded that Marston was entertaining his audience with traditional and familiar fare in *The Fawne*; and the geniality of the play supports his interpretation.

The Fawne, the lightest of Marston's plays, is filled with humor and high comedy, and it glints with irony rather than flashes with satire. It uses the same central situation as *The Malcontent*; for Faunus, like Malevole, is a duke in disguise, and from that vantage, he comments

126

on the court around him and sees that remedies are applied to some of its worst excesses. But Faunus is less personally involved than Malevole because he is in no danger, and, as a result, *The Fawne* offers quickness and excitement whereas *The Malcontent* offered urgency, fearfulness, and intensity.

The action in *The Fawne* is more limited, and the plot is less complicated than in the earlier play. Hercules, Duke of Ferrara and secure in his own power, presents himself at the court of Gonzago, Duke of Urbin, in the guise of Faunus, the last word in flattering courtiers, as a member of his son Tiberio's entourage. Tiberio has been sent ostensibly to woo Gonzago's daughter, Dulcimel, on his father's behalf; but his father hopes—and goes with his son to ensure—that the girl will shock his phlegmatic son from his unnatural aloofness and cause him to woo her for himself. Dulcimel is a high-spirited, intelligent girl who at once falls in love with Tiberio; and her campaign, with judicious aid from Faunus, awakens the young man to his own feelings, and all ends as Faunus wishes.

The major part of the play, however, is concerned with Faunus's own awakening to the extent of courtly corruption and hypocrisy and his efforts to deal with such behavior. He flatters the courtiers into actions so grostesque that, when he brings them to exposure as frauds, they feel a certain humiliation and are brought to a recognition of their folly. Grotesquerie is the mark of their behavior since Urbin's court is not full of Machiavellian intrigue as was Duke Pietro's; Urbin's is a brighter place where foibles and follies glitter like bubbles waiting to be pricked. Things once savagely bludgeoned are, in this play, gently encouraged to swell until they virtually burst themselves. Their traits are limned in their names.

Nymphadora professes to be the world's great lover; Herod Frappatore includes that claim amid a swaggering general assertion of superiority. His brother, Sir Amoroso Debile Dosso, the weak-backed one, is impotent; and his wife, Garbetza, the tart one, has deceived him with his brother. Zuccone, the jealous gull, is wed to Zoya, or Goia the jewel, whom he naturally misvalues. Lesser court figures hover around these central characters, and Hercules deals with the body of them at once but without complexity of plot. The activity is largely verbal; the courtiers are exploited sometimes singly and sometimes in groups. After early suspicions that Faunus might be a spy, they fall over themselves to tell him everything, so delighted are they to find him chiming so perfectly with all their thoughts and opinions: "Why that's my humor to the very thread, thou dost speak my proper thoughts" cries Nymphadora ecstatically and, in doing so, speaks for them all (2.176). Thus Faunus's revelation of them at the Parliament of Cupid is all the more effective; they can only admit their folly and wonder that "all inward, inward, he lurkt in the bosome of us, & yet wee know not his profession" (2.219).

The tone of the play is accurately caught by Cupid when he states the purpose of his Parliament: "to survay our old lawes, and punish their transgressions, for that continually the complaints of lovers ascend up to our deity, that love is abusde, and basely bought and solde, beautie corrupted, affection fainde, and pleasure her selfe sophisticated" (2.216). This stock theme is handled comically; fierce denunciations of lust, adultery, and sexual perversion are not heard. Marston makes his points quite clearly, but in a language that, without becoming coy or reticent, noticeably avoids powerful fulmination. The accused are portrayed cleverly and amusingly but not harshly. Their folly is obvious and is allowed to speak for itself.

The urbanity which marks much of the humor in *The Fawne* makes a first appearance in the Prologue which promises no hard attacks, no bawdry, but the "nymble forme of commody" showing "Meere spectacle of life, and publique manners" (2.145). Such modest promises lead to ever more fulsome praise of the audience's taste and manners. Just as this approach begins to sound like too great a change of heart for Marston, the audience is awakened into recognition of the falsity of the disarming view that they were being encouraged to take of themselves by the concluding couplet: "Now if that any wonder why he's drawn / To such base soothings, know his play's; *The Fawne*" (2.145). The method Faunus uses in the main action is neatly demonstrated on the theater audience so that they may the better appreciate its efficacy in the play itself: he lulls the victim by beguiling him with what he wants to hear and then plucks the supports from beneath him so that he falls into realizing the truth.

I *"The Nymble Form" of the Comedy*

The exposition is finely managed: Hercules explains to Renaldo why, having reached years of discretion, he should suddenly don a disguise and "breake forth / Those stricter Limits of regardfull state" (2.147). He reveals himself as an understanding father quite unlike the usual rigid disciplinarians of the seventeenth-century comic stage, but one not uncommon in Marston's plays. He is also Marstonian in his desire to place unnatural curbs upon himself no longer; for once in his life, albeit rather late, he has decided he will satisfy "wilde longings." Clearly this will not lead to any large-scale debauchery or to a series of escapades worthy of an Eulenspiegel. One of the ironies of the action is that Hercules' desire to try fresh fields results only in his learning how little he had known of those courtly ones where he had spent his life. Hercules' beliefs are the same that sustained Freevill in *The Dutch Curtezan*. Tiberio, indeed, is seemingly cut from the same cloth as Malheureux in his coldness toward women and in his denial of natural feelings. But, as Tiberio is not so rigid as Malheureux, Hercules does not have to go as far as Freevill in educating him. Hercules concisely expresses his belief in a soliloquy that harks back to the younger Marston in its glance at the old bogey of Opinion:

> He that doth strive to please the world's a foole.
> To have the fellowe crie, *O marke him, grave,*
> *See how austeerely he doth give example,*
> *Of repressed heate and steddy life*
> Whilest my fore'd life against the streame of bloud
> Is tugg'd along, and all to keepe the God
> Of fooles and women: *Nice opinion:*
> Whose strict preserving makes oft great men fooles
> And fooles oft great men: no thou world know thus,
> *"Ther's nothing free but it is generous."*
>
> (2.148)

When the scene switches to Urbin, the pace changes abruptly. The firm good sense of Hercules gives way to the light chatter of idle courtiers that is concerned with rumor and gossip about the forthcoming birthday festivities of Princess Dulcimel. News of Tiberio's arrival causes a further stir which is cut short by the entry of Gonzago and his court, followed almost at once by Tiberio and his train. Among the latter is Hercules who is disguised as Faunus. Gonzago, who is among Marston's best comic characters, is of the school of Polonius; but he has not Polonius's elusive grasp of political skills or of life's truisms: he is a Balurdo grown old and immensely self-approving. Words and phrases are his delight, and he is endlessly self-explanatory about his own nonexistent rhetorical art: however, his delight in himself is contagious: "Lah sir, thus men of braine can speake in cloudes / Which weake eyes cannot pearce" (2.173). The last and least sinning of all those to be tried at Cupid's court, he is oblivious to the last as he heartily condemns the crime for which he is to be tried immediately before his own case is heard. No man can speak better for himself, and his first words in the play place him with a certainty and a sparkle that testify to Marston's sure comic touch.

Kind at heart, Gonzago is nonetheless at the other extreme from the shrewd father that Hercules is. Gonzago looks on Tiberio and is deceived, and he thereby sets the pattern that he thereafter follows steadily:

> When thou shalt behold Tiberios life-full eyes
> and well-fild vaines, complection firme, and
> hayres that curles with the strength of lustie
> moysture, (I thinke wee yet can speake, wee ha
> beene eloquent) thou must shape thy thoughts /
> to apprehend his father well in yeeres, /
>> A grave wise Prince, whose beautie is his honour,
>> And well past life, and doe not give thy thoughts
>> Least libertie to shape a divers scope,
>> (My Lord *Granuffo:* pray ye note my phrase.)
>> So shalt thou not abuse thy younger hope.

(2.151)

The perfect foil to Gonzago's garrulity is the silent Granuffo, and his silence is seemingly born of years of futile attempts to break his master's flow.

Tiberio pleads his father's case as the future husband of Dulcimel with an honesty that is all the more shattering for being so well meant. Hercules' age is stressed as against Tiberio's youth. Thus, when Dulcimel ventures that the portrait of Hercules sent to her shows a man of some forty years, Tiberio politely corrects her: "Then it doth somewhat flatter, for our father hath seene more yeares, and is a little shrunke from the full strength of time" (2.153). Even Gonzago feels that this correction is a little chilly. It is an excellent scene: Gonzago exudes verbosity, Tiberio is dully polite; Hercules stands to one side receiving little comfort from anything he hears, or sees; and Dulcimel seems as yet to be no more than the conventionally attractive heroine.

She is to be discovered when next seen (after a considerable interlude for demonstrations by the court apes) to be vivacious and intelligent. She wants Tiberio, and she clearly can expect no help from Tiberio himself, who is funny because he is so slow and so unromantic a young man. As a result, Dulcimel cleverly uses her father as a go-between in the very affair he would do anything to frustrate, and she contrives plans which she reveals to her father as the shameless devices of Tiberio. Gonzago's anxiety to frustrate the supposed affair becomes the means of its being successful, for he faithfully passes on to a very gradually awakening Tiberio all the information about Dulcimel's feelings and plans. Dulcimel is of that group of confident, self-assured young women who willingly risk anything to find their love and to win him in marriage. A Crispinella without tartness, she is Marston's nearest approach to the Shakespearian romantic heroine.

Marston's handling of this sequence of events displays his subtle control of tone and structure. Dulcimel's artful assumption of her father's manner and her leading him by exquisite flattery to do her will and bring about a happy ending are neatly paralleled by the way Faunus flatters the courtiers by aping their puffy language so that eventually the extravagance of their own behavior undoes them and leads them to a cure. Considered not as Faunus but as Hercules, Hercules is matched with Gonzago; the latter misunderstands completely Dulcimel's purposes and is quite lost in a strange world. Hercules discovers himself to be in an unknown world but has the strenth of mind to recognize the fact and combat it.

The romance between Dulcimel and Tiberio is the mainspring of the play, but it does not dominate the action. In avoiding any scenes of romantic ardor between the young couple, Marston once more turns a liability into a comic yet sympathetic benefit to his entertainment. The lovers oddly have little to do with each other directly; by an amusing twist of convention, their love scenes and their declarations occur between father and daughter rather than between lover and beloved. Gonzago first draws Dulcimel's attention to the desirability of Tiberio; and her replies, or more properly her advances, to the young man are spoken, ironically, on her behalf by her father. Her ardor and Tiberio's passivity meet amusingly in the old man's garrulity. Tiberio says little when onstage with Dulcimel and he is the rather obtuse member of a lively group in which she displays all the brightness. Her lively wit and passion contrast amusingly with his stolid uprightness. Their union, however, is the standard against which the others in the play are to be measured; and Hercules' impressive expression of the sane and healthy attitude toward love and marriage (very like Dulcimel's) is the one statement against which the feelings of the others must be measured.

Tiberio is that awkward character, the uneager young man who is pursued. In Marston's eyes, Tiberio is unnatural for quite serious reasons as well as being handy for comic effectiveness, especially when he is found alongside such extremists in loving as Nymphadora and his fellows. His stolidity is the despair of his father. Tiberio is not a convincing lover and hero at first sight, but he stands in no danger of forfeiting affection in the manner that Bertram does, for example, in *All's Well That Ends Well*. Tiberio gradually warms to his task and never despises or scorns his father; this loyalty is perhaps as surprising as Hercules' original generosity, but it may well reflect Marston's serious view of family loyalty and affection. This relationship gives a color to the action that is sentimental in the truest sense of the word, and it allows the audience to laugh at Tiberio but never to deride or dislike him.

II   *The Exposure of Court Follies*

While the comic crosses of this true love are revealed, the courtiers' wilder follies and excesses are displayed in a series of stories or situations that are linked by general theme and atmosphere rather than by any ordered narrative, and, very importantly, by the person of Faunus. After Hercules arrives in Urbin, he does not have to exert himself to put the courtiers through their paces. Lacking the urgent impetus of Malevole and not threatened in any such dangerous way as he was, Hercules works quietly; and part of his strength lies in his being so quiet and so calm a worker. He guides, encourages, and goads his victims in the ways on which they are bound. Personal rancor is not Hercules' driving force, for he has suffered no personal loss or disgrace. He works upon principle alone rather than upon principle reinforced by personal suffering. Hercules is not a malcontent who is battling evil and seeking revenge. The extent and corrupting power of flattery does shock him into a declaration of revenge upon all who offend, but he is not driven to it by the broader compulsive energy that usually drives malcontents or satirists.

Hercules promises revenge less harsh than Malevole's but, for all that, a no less effective one. Revenge of the traditional bloodthirsty kind is a matter for comedy in *The Fawne*. Only Zuccone, the ludicrously jealous husband, roars like the conventional wronged man: "I will be most tirannous, blooddily tirannous in my revenge, and most terrible in my curses" (2.167). Coming from him, this raises laughter, not shudders. Elsewhere, Herod, after some braggadocio about playing the Italian, says, "*Nymphadora* in direct phrase, thou shouldst murther the Prince, so revenge thine owne wronges, and be rewarded for that revenge." Faunus takes him up: "Afore the light of my eyes, I thinke I shall admire, wonder at you. What? ha ye plots, projects, correspondences, and stratagems? why are not you in better place?" (2.162). Herod, as usual, is playing the blusterer; and neither he nor Nymphadora is aware of the sarcasm in Faunus's fulsome approval of their suggestions and in his amazement at their still low place in society. When Zuccone enters to be twitted by all three, Faunus jovially asks: "Plots ha you laid? inductions daungerous?" (2.164). These are the clichés of revenge plays and here Marston tosses them about briskly and wittily.

When Hercules speaks seriously of revenge, it is not in passion but with an earnestness and a right reason that are forceful and impressive:

> I will revenge us all upon you all
> With the same stratagem, we still are caught,
> Flatterie it selfe: and sure all knowes the sharpenesse
> Of reprehensive language is even blunted
> To full contempt; since vice is now term'd fashion
> And most are growne to ill even with defence
> I vow to wast this most prodigious heat
> That fals into my age, like scorching flames
> In depth of numb'd December, in flattering all
> In all of their extreamest vitiousnesse,
> Till in their own lov'd race they fall most lame,
> And meet full butte, the close of Vices shame.
>
> (2.158)

Hercules is moved to this declaration when he discovers how easily and eagerly his animadversions against his supposed Lord Tiberio and Tiberio's father are heard by Herod and Nymphadora. He hears them vie in insult, calling him in his real role, "that old doting iniquitie of age, that only eyed lecherous Duke" (1.157). He soon discovers that the whole court is rotten; for the courtiers, from Gonzago down, comprise the extravagant figures who are the stock targets for the satirist; but they are freshly sketched in this play.

The court fantastics perform some familiar comic turns with great sprightliness and edge. Herod, for instance, makes the old mistake of pretending that letters of a common sort are actually of a rarer sort. His embarrassment is compounded by the fact that his reading is

overheard by the sister-in-law whom he had seduced and whom he
describes in the letter with an amusing directness which does not
appeal to her. Garbetza's punishment is to learn what Herod really
thinks of her when she, in her pride, had imagined she was his only
love. Thus Marston exploits the scene for a double purpose.

Zuccone's humbling is more direct: after playing the part of the
burlesque jealous husband, he is made to swing to the other extreme
and plead with absurd humbleness for forgiveness by following his
wife across the stage on his knees. On two occasions, when the other
courtiers gather to deride him in chorus, their attacks rise to a
crescendo in which by swift turn they hurl one-word insults at him;
but their explosion of verbal barbs is abruptly ended by their rushing
from the stage. The typically Marstonian exercise in verbal
techniques combines with stagecraft in this unusual way twice in the
play (2.171; 2.203–4).

III   *The Comic Effects of Voices and Language*

In a prefatory letter, addressed to his "equall Reader," Marston
stressed the fact that *The Fawne* was "a Comedie, whose life rests
much in the Actors voice." He meant, as he reiterated at the end of
his letter, that the life of a play consisted in action: it was meant to be
heard and seen, not merely read. However, we may take his phrase
more literally than perhaps he meant it in a play whose variety of
spoken language is so various and so skillfully deployed. Gonzago and
Granuffo mark the poles of ceaseless talk and of hardly broken
silence, and Dulcimel and Tiberio mark a similar polarity on a slightly
less extreme level. Hercules stands midmost as the man of two voices;
he is sober and quiet as Hercules and flatteringly smooth and guileful
as Faunus. The courtiers clearly affect accents to match their
manners: Herod, the Bobadil manner; Nymphadora, all a fluttering,
fake exquisiteness; and Zuccone, either shouts in high rage or whines
in humble pleading. At times, Marston virtually orchestrates these
sounds; and their distinctive timbres and manners ring against each
other throughout the play.

This vivacity of language carries splendidly through to the last act
and to the Parliament of Cupid where everything is presented in the
formal jargon of the law court. The Parliament allows Marston to deal
in another way with the problem of the comedy finale in which some
lessons must be applied and the purposes of the commentator and

organizer fulfilled; for, when Cupid effectively treats the characters by bringing them in turn before the bar, successive accusations and sentences emphasize the types and their punishments. "Against the plurality of Mistresses" (2.217) brings Nymphadora to face all the ladies to whom he had sworn allegiance. "An act against counterfeiting of *Cupids* royall coine" (2.218) brings in Sir Amoroso to be humiliatingly dismissed with "in thy ignorance be quietly happie" (2.219). His brother faces charges under the heading "forgers of love letters, false braggarts of ladies favours" (2.219), confesses precipitately, and is dismissed to the ship of fools to be ducked twice a day.

Zuccone, a slanderer and "lewde defamer" (2.219) of ladies, meets the only happy sentence when Zoya proves as good as her name and reveals that her wild behavior was a pretense to bring him to his senses; he forswears jealousy in the future and is reunited with her, but his contrition is emphasized by his lengthy process in court.

Thus follies and absurdities are exposed; humiliation is added to repentance; and each of the accused recognizes his own folly, even Gonzago, though it naturally takes him longer than anyone else: "By the Lord I am ashamde of my selfe, that's the plain troth, but I know now wherefore this Parliament was: what a slumber have I been in?" (2.224). Such a perception may well be a good fixative for repentance: "Thus few strike saile untill they run on shelfe,/ The eye sees all thinges but his proper selfe" (2.206).

The Fawne justifies the Prologue's claims for its nimbleness and even its gracefulness; the play is one of sprightliness and energetic sobriety. The themes are old ones and are staged with great assurance and facility. The mark of *The Fawne* is control; Marston is less strident but not less forceful and direct. The mood of the play still allows place for Hercules' censure of courtly life. His disquisitions on general social ills and, more trenchantly, on women, lawyers, drinking, children, and love are apt since they are balanced by the comical extravagances of the court. The two love stories move forward steadily, both under the competent guidance of women. The physical action tends to be concentrated in these two love stories, and nearly all the action concerned with Tiberio and Dulcimel is clearly fitted into the inter-act musical entertainment. The invention nowhere falters.

If Finkelpearl is correct about the Inns' Christmas entertainment having been a shaping force for this play, Marston demonstrates his willingness and his ability to fashion traditional shows to his own ends. In this respect, his growth between *Histriomastix* and *The Fawne* in technical assurance in manipulating such older forms is impressive. In five years, he had learned a great deal about staging "comical satyres." With such development and with such natural gifts, it is the greater loss that this comedy was his last one; he was now to write the tragedy, *Sophonisba*.

CHAPTER 9

The Wonder of Women or
The Tragedie of Sophonisba

M ARSTON chose "words well senc'd, best suting subject grave"
(Epil. 2.68) for *Sophonisba*, a tragedy of a more orthodox kind
than anything else he wrote. And yet, being Marston, he makes of the
tragic form something that is quite his own. Despite its battles, its
murderous political intrigues, its sexual violence, and its darkly
melodramatic witchcraft, the overall impression that the play leaves
is one of formality and of steady-paced ceremonial. An occasional
sardonic flash is all that Marston allows his satirical comical genius in
this story which is taken from the history of the war between Carthage
and Rome. In plainest terms it tells of the enduring love of
Sophonisba for Massinissa, the great Carthaginian general, in the face
of harsh tests and fierce obstacles; a love that eventually leads her to
take poison so that Massinissa, having been betrayed by the rulers of
Carthage, can keep his faith both with his new Roman allies and with
his wife by delivering her up to the conquering Roman general,
Scipio.

Marston mocked the fictions of his plot in *Antonio and Mellida,* but
in *Sophonisba* he is serious. In fact, Marston's remarkable achievement in this play is the address and force with which he handles his
plot to win spectacular theatricality and powerful emotional dramatic
impact. Sophonisba and Massinissa test the stoic quality against the
corruption of the world; but, whereas previous tests in Marston's
plays had been carried out in a wild and savage world where farce
jostled tragedy and where inane fools rubbed shoulders with
corrosive madmen, the scene in *Sophonisba* is pragmatic and Roman;
court frivolities are banished; the enemy is more frightening because
he is more calculating. The changes of party and abandoment of
loyalties are brutally logical and politically expedient, not mere
courtiers' steps danced by a Balurdo or by a Bilioso.

In this world, the grand gesture of Massinissa's joining Sophonisba in a suicide pact is not even considered because it would be a romantic gesture. Theirs is no romantic passion for which, like Antony and Cleopatra, they would sacrifice the world. Their love is stated and accepted without illimitable ardor, but it is firmly evoked. The climax of their love is, characteristically, unlike that of any other such couple; but it is true to the development of the play's argument. Other endings of Marston's plays have been not quite what was expected; but, in *Sophonisba*, the tenor of the play makes the unexpected ending satisfactory.

Toughness and hard simplicity are symbolic of the play's essential qualities. For men, there is only adherence to self and principle. Marston always proclaimed the creed that one must be oneself, and in this play he works it out in strict terms that leave no room for compromise or maneuver to the man of integrity and honor. "Speach makes us men, and thers no other bond / Twixt man and man, but words" (2.22). Or, as Gelosso—Massinissa's one loyal friend in Carthage—says, foreshadowing Coriolanus, "And wee shall hate faith-breakers worse then man-eaters" (2.23).

I   *The Matching of Theatrical Spectacle and Tragic Argument*

Marston himself sets out the argument of his play in the Prologue:

> A gratefull hearts just height; Ingratitude
> And vowes base breach with worthy shame persu'd.
> A womans constant love as firm as fate
> A blamelesse Counsellor well borne for state
> The folly to inforce free love, These know
> This subject with full light doth amply show.
>
> (2.6)

A restrained but powerful manner will give fresh expression in *Sophonisba* to familiar ideas from Marston. In "sceans exempt from ribaldrie or rage" (as the Epilogue calls them) but in ones by no means bare of theatrical spectacle and bold contrasts, the argument of the play is forcefully acted out.

The theatrical spectacle begins with the Prologue, for the speaker of it is ushered in by eleven characters attended by eight pages, with torches and weapons, and divided into two groups. One group, large and festively solemn, consists of the Carthaginian nobility led by Sophonisba and Massinissa; the other group, smaller but ominous, consists of Syphax (a rejected suitor of Sophonisba's), his attendant, Vangue, and two pages. The Prologue briefly introduces the characters in the tableau. The mood is not jubilant but severe, and the audience is left to muse on the significance of the closing couplet: *"For just worth never rests on popular frowne, / To have done well is faire deeds onely crowne"* (2.8).

The stage clears; and Syphax, left with Vangue, asserts himself a vengeful villain. He is a Mendoza made fearful because he is a stronger man and has no hint of the grotesque in his character. He recognizes the unreasonableness of his anger, springing as it does from unrequited love; but he defiantly claims that this passion gives him unlimited scope. Like others in the play, he speaks with a ferocious directness: *"Passion is Reason when it speakes from Might"* (2.11). He determines to join his forces with those of Scipio.

This armed man with his paean of malevolent egoism gives way to the bridal chamber where Sophonisba muses on the traditional behavior expected of the bride:

> the Bride must steale
> Before her Lord to bed: and then delaies,
> Long expectations, all against knowne wishes.
> I hate these figures in locution,
> These about phrases forc'd by *ceremonie;*
> We must still seeme to flie what we most seeke
> And hide our selves from what we faine would find us.
>
> (2.11)

In this speech, arguments from *The Scourge of Villanie* about direct speech and opinions of Crispinella about frankness in love talk are knit together gracefully so that a softer side of Sophonisba's nature, otherwise little touched upon, is marked without any hint of the salacity so frequent on these occasions. At the same time, her words show her liking for discussion, a trait shared by most of the major characters in the play. Music announces the arrival of Massinissa and of the masquers who dance and sing in honor of Hymen, but the wedding-night mood, already darkened by the shadows thrown by Syphax, is quite broken by the news of Scipio's approach. Duty calls Massinissa to arms and, when he leaves, he is encouraged by Sophonisba's selfless desire to be a soldier's wife "that valews his renoune above faint pleasures" (2.18).

The first act trenchantly sets out the theme of selfishness versus self-denial, and it emphasizes this opposition by staging which insists continually on visual contrasts. The opening tableau, divided richly about the figures of the Prologue, falls away to the energetic evil of Syphax, "armd from top to toe"; this scene gives way to the bridal chamber—all silks and soft furnishings, Sophonisba in her night-gown, the wedding party gaily clad, the whole set off by the fantastic dance of Cupids and the rousing song to Hymen. At the height of the celebration, Carthalon enters, "his sword drawne, his body wounded, his shield strucke full of darts: *Massin.* being reddy for bedde." The last direction is important, for the mood turns back to masculine violence and war, and Massinissa leaves only to return "arm'd a cape a pee." The act closes not with speeches of nuptial love but with declarations of self-denial that allow Sophonisba to emerge as the central figure who offsets and balances the opening statements of Syphax. Conventional devices are used with facility in the act—the villain's soliloquy of self-revelation, the preparations for the wedding night, the masque, the descriptive battle speech of Carthalon—but the devices serve a dramatic purpose and are not merely theatrical spectacles.

Act 1 introduces the main characters; act 2, the political world they inhabit. At the close of the first act, Massinissa loftily refused oaths of loyalty: "I was not borne so small to doubt or feare" (2.17). The dangers of such idealism now emerge too clearly. The Carthaginian leaders wish to buy Syphax back by offering him Sophonisba and by leaving Massinissa to be poisoned by Gisco. They argue with brutal directness for expediency: "how so ere nice vertue censures of it, / He hath the grace of warre, that hath wars profit" (2.20). Gelosso rejects this sophistry with nobility:

> I am bound to loose
> My life but not my honour for my country;
> Our vow, our faith, our oath, why th'are our selves,
> And he thats faithlesse to his proper selfe
> May be excused if he breake faith with princes.
>
> (2.21)

Nonetheless, the world of realpolitik grinds on; and Sophonisba, though equally horrified, has to submit under urgent protest to its will.

The betrayal of Massinissa is, inevitably, followed at once by his appearance; he is wounded but is singing his country's praises. Gisco fails in his task and is dismissed by Massinissa with a flash of the savagely comic: "Gisco, th'art old, / Tis time to leave off murder."

Massinissa will not have him put to death because "the God-like part of Kings is to forgive" (2.26). Learning of the treachery, he caps this show of mercy with an equally impressive one of courage in adversity by refusing to rage or whine; he instead plans to do battle with his enemies. The treacheries of the Carthaginians fall on their own heads when Syphax, anxious to reach Sophonisba, hurries off and leaves his army to be decimated by Massinissa. Gisco and Gelosso are executed, but such action is as useless as it is cruel. The counselors are last seen in a fury of recrimination and abject fear.

This act moves swiftly, but its excitement and activity do not mask the dramatic forcefulness of its debate about the qualities of loyalty and endurance. What slight comedy there is, is harsh; and the amusement caused by the panic-stricken senators is shot through with scorn because these men could never be mistaken for bubbles, such as Herod Frappatore, nor could their plans be his empty braggadocio.

The energies of the play now gather more quickly to a head as the main characters are subjected to yet more stringent tests of their quality. Sophonisba rejects every advance of Syphax when she is forced to face him in his palace. He descends, futilely, to physical violence against her and, in final desperation, seeks the aid of the witch, Erictho. In the most startling theatrical scene in the play, she tricks him into sleeping with her by assuming the form of Sophonisba. He takes his sword to her but she vanishes like a wraith. Marston, piling on the supernatural spectacle, introduces the ghost of Sophonisba's father, Asdrubal, whom Syphax dismisses contemptuously because he learns from him nothing of the future. Syphax is defeated in personal combat by Massinissa, but he still nourishes his hatred of Sophonisba and Massinissa. His blending of truth into his malign arguments is at once fascinating and horrifying, for he praises Sophonisba's staunchness to Carthage and her power to influence only because he wishes to convince Scipio that she will make Massinissa break his oath of allegiance with the Romans. In the world of this play, virtue is its own reward in the hardest way.

The action moves to its climax. Massinissa is poised between his oath of duty to Scipio and his oath of love to Sophonisba when Scipio demands that he hand his wife over to the guardianship of Rome. Sophonisba resolves his dilemma by drinking poisoned wine "for honor and just faith / Are most true Gods, which we should much adore" (2.61). In the final tableau, her body is brought before Scipio and a viciously despondent Syphax as a symbol of the constancy that is

the theme of the play. Scipio speaks a conventional epitaph, but
Massinissa adds one that is quite Marstonian:

> Thou whome like sparkling steele the strokes of Chance
> Made hard and firme; and like wild fier turnd
> The more cold fate, more bright thy vertue burnd,
> And in the whole seas of miseries didst flame.
> On thee lov'd creature of a deathlesse fame
> Rest all my honour.
>
> (2.63)

This stress on the fierce quality of Sophonisba's constancy reaffirms a
Marstonian view of stoicism. Mere patience is not enough; man's
nature is not to be repressed in marmoreal calm; for the serenity won
by the admired stoic comes by way of vigorous trials. The wild
outburst that marked the abandonment of placid acquiescence in
earlier plays gives way to a relentless, steadier action that com-
prehends Massinissa's conflict with Syphax, as well as Sophonisba's
struggle against treachery and her bold efforts to thwart Syphax.
Significantly, blood is not demanded for blood; and, just as Malevole
was disinterested in simple revenge killing, Massinissa spares Gisco
and Syphax. The stoic heroes in this play are carved not in marble but
in "sparkling steele."

II *Marston's Achievement in* Sophonisba

Characters are divided into good and evil; the spectacle and the
action are likewise after the fashion of the tableau and recall Marston's
interest in morality play structures. The richness of setting and
decoration is, however, handled more to evoke formality than to
create lavish shows and activity. There is an "intention to achieve
simple massiveness here through a straightforward illustration of
stoic virtue."[1] That massiveness is enlivened by the energy—the need
to act rather than merely to endure—that Marston sees as a vital part
of his ideal of stoic virtue. This energy informs the language, the
characters, and the action.

The poetry is better and more evenly sustained in *Sophonisba* than
anywhere else in Marston. The debate between the false Carthaginian rulers and Gelosso in the second act shows authority and
achievement:

> GEL: Politique Lord, speake low! tho heaven beares
> A face far from us, Gods have most long eares,
> *Jove* has a hundred marble marble hands.
> CARTHALON: O I, in Poetry or Tragique sceane.
> GEL: I feare Gods onely know what Poets mean.
> CAR: Yet heare me: I will speake close truth and cease,
> Nothing in Nature is unservisable,
> No, not even *Inutility* it selfe,
> Is then for nought dishonesty in beeing,
> And if it be somtimes of forced use,
> Wherein more urgent then in saving nations?
>
> (2.20–21)

The astringent humor of Carthalon's scathing dismissal of the gods' revenge to "Poetry or Tragique sceane" is a good example of how Marston can sardonically remind the audience of the mingled reality and unreality of the stage world. In the last act, Syphax's exultations when Sophonisba is carried in are cut off by Massinissa with four curt words: "Starve thy leane hopes" (2.63). Such thrusts help prevent the main figures from seeming to be cardboard types. Indeed, Sophonisba, Massinissa, and Syphax, though they clearly represent definite attitudes, do not become mere mouthpieces of them.

Marston never permits the play to become a mere forum of debate on stoical ideals. The pacing of the exchanges, the occasional down-to-earth remarks, and the sharper flashes give a crackle to the dialogue. Sophonisba is always what the main title of the play terms her, "The Wonder of Women"; but, when necessary, she shows a sharp grasp of political realities. Ironically, her prescience about practical politics and intrigues is well-founded but is an insufficient defense for herself. She is rightly wary of all servants, especially of her maid Zanthia; but she is nonetheless betrayed by her: "Their Lorde's their gaine: and he that most will give / With him (they will not dye: but) they will live." (2.36).

Sophonisba is a satisfying play: its characters, its poetry, its theatrical accomplishments are turned to one end; and the relentless logic of the argument moves irresistibly to the implacable climax. Sophonisba and Massinissa act throughout with such authority and energy that they cannot rouse affection, perhaps not even warm sympathy; but they command, in every sense of the word, the best kind of admiration. Marston created a fine stage climax while keeping an honesty in his argument that few dramatists would have cared to risk. His tragedy is consummated with only one dignified death, and the effect is won out of simplicity. In the beginning of his career, Marston had used the old device of the solemn entry of a dead body for comic effect; and one more mark of his growing security with stage devices is that he could so movingly and fittingly end his only tragedy with so convincing a use of this device.

III   Marston and Music

In Marston's last complete play, he aptly draws attention to one aspect of his art which he felt especially thrust upon him: "After all, let me intreat my Reader not to taxe me, for the fashion of the Entrances and Musique of this Tragidy, for know it is printed onely as it was presented by youths, & after the fashion of the private stage" (2.64). The youths were trained musicians, and it was the fashion of both the private and the public stages to use music in their performances. Music was one traditional ingredient among many of theatrical entertainments, and, in the tough commercial world Marston worked in, it would have been foolish not to trade on the musical advantages the youths had over the adults. Burbage recognized them when he explained away the additions his company made to *The Malcontent* as needed "to entertaine a little more time, and to abridge the not received custome of musicke in our Theater" (1.143). The production that this disclaimer introduced showed that the received customs of music at the Globe were, in fact, ample. They did not, however, offer the range of opportunity that was available to Marston when he wrote *Sophonisba*. "The fashion of the private stage" was something that Marston had to accept, but fashion did not completely rule him since he had an effect on it.

Music can evoke any emotion at any pitch and do so more quickly than the spoken word. This power has always been gratefully recognized in the theater: "the play without any music was unheard of until about the last quarter of the nineteenth century, when musicless drama began to make its own way."[2] Marston was well aware that music could suggest courtly power and opulence, swell "three rusty swords" into an army, make of a few dancers a swirling ball. In every way music aided him in emphasizing the interplay of emotion, the clashes of mood, and the contrasts which were an important part of his dramatic technique. Sensitive as he was to the appearance of his stage plays in print, Marston may have felt that the rich directions for music printed in *Sophonisba* read awkwardly. The calls for music in this play are not unusual, but the details of the instrumentation of it are. However, as Marston chooses to mention fashion's imperatives in his note, it is only fair to notice how well he organizes them to his own dramatic ends.

His note draws attention to the union between himself as dramatist and as the producer of his play in the theater. He calls for music at a particular moment in his action, but he notes that the actual music is provided by another hand. In act 1, "foure boyes antiquely attiered with bows and quivers dauncing to the *Cornets*" sing a choral song to Hymen which is set for "cornets, Organ, and voices" (2.12). Whether Marston disclaims the precise musical instrumentation or merely the manner in which the directions are ultimately fulfilled, the carefully prepared effect made by the music in the action is his. For example, the action has heightened impact when dainty mock fighting to music is interrupted by Carthalon's bloody entrance and by the eruption of real war. The inter-act music after act 1—"Cornets and Organs playing loud full Musicke"—aptly heralds a second act shot through with battle calls on cornets. When the third act concentrates on Syphax's attempts to seduce Sophonisba, "Organ mixt with Recorders for this Act" makes music that contrasts with the mood created by the violent opening to the act's events: "*Sypha* his dagger twon about her háire drags in *Sophonisba* in hir nightgowne petticoate" (2.32).

A second reversal of mood in the third act depends on music. Sophonisba's absolute faithfulness to Massinissa in the face of every threat moves even Syphax, and he allows her to offer a sacrifice to Massinissa's memory. This is celebrated with "Cornets and Organs playing full musick" and a blank song. Structurally, it separates the violent wooing of Syphax from the skillful trickery which Sophonisba immediately uses to escape him: it forms a solemn interlude between bouts of hectic action. That the song is "blank" does not mean that Marston did not care what song was sung, but that the particular song he had in mind for that spot, whether it was one he had written himself or not, has not survived (2.36). Probably the words were given to the musicians and became music-room property, and, like many another song, was not available for the printer.

The musical crux of the play is the fourth act, which most closely approaches the operatic in the infernal business with Erictho. The inter-act music is of "Organs, Violls and Voices," the first time viols are used; and their use may be a clue about the "infernall musique" which "plaies softly whilst Erictho enters and when she speakes ceaseth" (2.46). She promises to force "The ayre to musicke, and the shads of night / To forme sweete sounds" (2.48). When she vanishes to prepare her illusion, "Infernall Musique softly" is again heard. Syphax is overawed by the eerie music which gives way to a completely different sound when "a treble Violl and a base Lute play softly within the Canopy" and he himself marks the change:

> Harke, harke, now softer melody strikes mute
> Disquiet nature: O thou power of sound
> How thou dost melt me. Harke, how even Heaven
> Gives up his soule amongst us . . . . .
> Harke: shee coms,
>   *A short song to soft Musique above*
> Now nuptiall Hymes inforced Spirits sing
>   *Cantant*

(2.49–50)

When Erictho appears in the shape of Sophonisba, Syphax cries ecstatically: "Now Hell and Heaven ringes / With Musique spight of *Phoebus*" (2.50).

Two musical conventions combine in this scene: quiet, eerie music for supernatural events and sweet music for romance; and these kinds of music match the uneasy duality of the action. As this soft music for a blasphemous love quietly plays, the audience would naturally recall the simpler, happier love music heard in the first act.

This ingratiating love music lulls Syphax and brings him from fearful awe to confident romantic ardor. Tension continues through the inter-act music which is scored for "A Base Lute and a Treble Violl," instruments already linked with lovemaking (2.51). As the final act opens, Syphax rises marvelously confident in the fulfillment of his ardor; and he pulls back the bed-curtains to find he has lain with Erictho and has begotten a demon. The music has so built up the passionate mood that this revelation has a tremendous theatrical effect. There plays over all, of course, the irony that this music betokening love covers the worst kind of lust, the coupling of man and witch. In these scenes, Marston so accepts the conditions of his theater to display his craftsmanship to the full that the scene almost justifies itself on musical grounds alone.

More effects come, however. The jar of discovery which jerks Syphax back to earth is sharpened by the distant sounds of "A march far off" (2.53). The battle scene is pierced continually by marches and by the cornets; and, as the battle wanes, the sounds fade until they are heard "afar off sounding a charge" (2.57) when Sophonisba reappears. But the music swells again "sounding a march" to herald the arrival of Massinissa in his armor. On their first meeting since their interrupted wedding-night, the couple seems to hear again that night's quiet music; for Massinissa remarks: "Stay the sword./ Let slaughter cease, Sounds soft as Ledas breast /(stage direction for *Soft Musique*) Slide through all eares, this night be loves high feast" (2.58).

The volatile seventeenth-century audience readily responded to emotional appeal, and Marston boldly relied upon this reaction. Although the use of music in the theater was traditional, although the power of such effects as following brash musical flourishes with softer sounds from wind instruments or from strings was recognized, Marston's particular skill in harnessing music to the needs of his play was notable. He relies upon music's ability not only to create a mood but to control the intensity of feeling of that mood. The demands made upon an audience by the strong and changing passions of the closing scenes of *Sophonisba* are made bearable by the music that is heard. Marston sets a muted scene against a fiercer one wherein Massinissa is commanded to hand over Sophonisba to Scipio. She dies; and, as she is borne out, the sound of "Cornets, A March, Enter *Scipio* in full state triumphal ornamentes carried before him" is heard (2.61). In contrast to this ostentatious entry, soon after "Orgaine and Recorders play to a single voice: Enter in the mean time the mournful solemnity of *Massinissas* presenting *Sophon.* body" (2.63). The comparison of the two entries asserts a Marstonian method which aurally points the major theme of the play—the triumph of stoic endurance over violent endeavor.

Sophonisba, with its unusually full directions for music and range of musical effects, gives a rare opportunity to see and, as it were, hear a private theater play under the craftsmanship of Marston, for not all of the music in his plays is so carefully tailored to dramatic needs. In the lighter comedies especially, music can enter somewhat casually. For example, the morris dance in the first act of *Jacke Drum's Entertainment* has no purpose other than to show Sir Edward's generosity in allowing it. At other times, effrontery disarms criticism as it does in *What You Will*, when, after a rattle of cross-talk between pages, one says: "And so gentle *Appollo* touch thy nimble string, our sceane is donne yet fore wee cease wee sing" (2.273). "The breefe and semiquaver of it is we must [sing]" (1.22) is the cry of the young actors—or of their manager—and certainly of their audience. Marston usually manages the use of music so that the demand is made by his play as much as by his actors and their audience.

CHAPTER 10

Marston's Accomplishment

I Marston's Links with his Fellow Dramatists

IN 1633, John Marston, an elderly retired clergyman, may well have felt that twenty-five years' dedication to God's ministry was poorly commemorated by the reissue of six plays of his young manhood, no matter how anxiously their editor proclaimed their moral virtue.[1] Certainly, the plays in *Works of John Marston* were not the contribution by which Marston wished to be remembered, since he probably wanted little, if anything, to do with the theater. If he did so desire, his wish was frustrated, for his name was removed from the pages of the collection but not from the history of the theater in his era.

Had Marston, in his retirement, visited the theater, he would have glimpsed, even behind the polished surface of Caroline tragedy and tragicomedy, pale ghosts from his plays. The stage history of his plays between 1608 and 1642 belies, however, the extent of his historical dramatic influence. Only one performance of his plays—that of *The Malcontent* in 1635—is recorded;[2] but our knowledge of the theatrical calendar of those years is fragmentary. Moreover, it is quite unlikely that Marston's distinctive voice was heard only once in over thirty years when its echoes could be heard so frequently in the plays of Webster, Tourneur, Fletcher, Ford, Middleton, Shirley, and others. Instead, the fact that the editor of the collection of 1633 thought it a worthwhile commercial project to reprint six of his plays is a testimony to their vitality; for, at that time, only Jonson and Shakespeare among Marston's old professional colleagues had had such collections of their works published.[3] This factor is not an indication of Marston's place in seventeenth-century drama, but it is a seventeenth-century estimate of Marston's importance.

Force of circumstance made playwrights gregarious, socially and

149

artistically, in Marston's day. They plied their trade in a hard market. Ideas, themes, situations, words, were not private properties: "However jealously individual plays might be guarded by companies, there was no property in the rapidly-developing dramatic art of the writers."[4] One aspect of the War of the Theaters is of personal and commercial rivalries, of attack and counterattack; but another aspect is that the same playwrights who fought each other worked in ever-changing collaborations, wrote for different companies and different theaters, and applied what they learned in one place in another. "Both the untalented conventional writers and those with original creative gifts profited from this situation. They learned from each other, adapting, imitating and absorbing each other's original achievements as they appeared."[5]

When Marston began writing plays, what he had read and what he had seen acted helped shape what he wrote. He had an educated Elizabethan's knowledge of the Classics: the story of *Pigmalion's Image* comes from Ovid; his satires prove his acquaintance with Juvenal, Persius, and Horace among the satirists and with Epictetus (who supplies him with mottoes for the first three of the *Certaine Satyres*), Aristotle, and Seneca among the philosophers. He would have read Plautus and Terence and have had some living knowledge of them because of the translation of their themes, characters, and situations into Elizabethan comedy.[6]

How wide Marston's acquaintance with earlier English drama was, can only be surmised. His plays frequently reflect the form of the morality play, and he could have seen moral civic drama in Coventry, such as the last performance of the Corpus Christi Cycle there in 1579. He was not quite three years old then, but he was the age to be impressed, however, in 1584 and 1591 when the civic authorities at Coventry joined with the guilds and performed the extravagantly and extraordinarily expensively mounted play, *The Destruction of Jerusalem*. The Marston home faced onto Cross Cheaping, the central market and acting area in the city; and, as an important civic dignitary, John Marston, Sr. might have approved his son's watching an edifying play. Marston, between 1584 and 1592, would also have had opportunity, if not permission, to witness performances by fifty-two companies of touring players paid by the City Council for acting in Coventry.

At Oxford, he could also have seen plays in both Latin and English; but London afforded him the richest variety of plays to see and the

most avid playgoers—as he notes in the most cheerful satire,
"Humours," in *The Scourge of Villanie:*

> *Luscus* what's playd to day? faith now I know
> I set thy lips abroach, from whence doth flow
> Naught but pure *Juliat* and *Romio*
> ·································
> H'ath made a common-place booke out of plaies
> And speakes in print, at least what ere he sayes
> Is warranted by Curtaine *plaudeties.*
> ·································
> He writes, he railes, he jests, he courts, what not,
> And all from out his huge long scraped stock
> Of well penn'd playes.
>
> (SV, 11.37–51)

Luscus is condemned for the use to which he puts his playgoing, not
for frequenting the theaters. Luscus can only parrot what he sees and
hears; Marston, however, who was as knowledgeable as Luscus about
"what's playd today," had a professional playwright's "common-place
booke," but he was no lazy copier. He took notes in order to alter
what he witnessed, for what he borrowed he made his own.

He took note of Marlowe's ringing dramatic verse, which was an
exciting break from the old-fashioned formal tragic speech. Marlowe's
verse inspired many, but Marston is ready to mock its excesses
(albeit kindly) in *Antonio and Mellida* (1.7)—a play whose two-part
structure has its model in Marlowe's *Tamburlaine.* The brash yoking
of tragedy and farce in Marlowe's *Dr. Faustus* was less distasteful to
Elizabethan audiences at the Rose than to modern critics, and it
struck a responsive chord in Marston's imagination. Kyd's *Spanish
Tragedy* was extraordinarily popular and phrases from it quickly
passed into the common mythology of the stage; a recent study lists
fifty-nine plays between 1591 and 1638 that refer to Kyd's play. As for
Marston, he refers directly to it in *Antonio and Mellida* and in *The
Malcontent* (and it is also mentioned in *Eastward Hoe* and *Satiromastix*), but its influence as a shaper of revenge tragedy is most strongly
felt in *Antonio's Revenge* (as has been noted) in which Marston's own
reshaping of given material can be studied.[7]

Kyd's *The Spanish Tragedy* provides a model for Marston for the
court setting, the ruthless intrigues, the violence; Kyd's Hieronimo,
the revenger who stood in general Elizabethan dramatic imagination

as the great example of outraged fatherhood put in an impossible position, is the pattern for Andrugio in *Antonio's Revenge*. Hieronimo is the central figure, and it is essentially his tragedy that is presented. Andrugio is not the dominant figure in Marston's play; indeed, for a tragedy, it rather follows the pattern of a comedy and disperses its attention among several characters. It is less the story of Andrugio, or anyone else, than the story or depiction of court corruption and vice. Marston is less interested than Kyd in his narrative and in the opportunities that certain episodes offer for displaying conflicting attitudes and reactions. Revenge tragedy becomes the forum for debate on the themes and motives of the genre.

Whereas Kyd's framework is moral and presents implacable judges promising certain judgment about the issues in the play, Marston's framework is significantly theatrical and has actors sitting in judgment about the artifices of the theater. This concern causes the Induction to part 1 of *Antonio and Mellida* to cover some aspects of part 2 of Marston's play, but the discussion of acting and theatricality instituted in that Induction is intermittently carried on in the play (Piero's concern with his own feigning, Balurdo's trouble with his beard). Kyd accepts the genre of revenge tragedy and plays it to the hilt; Marston, characteristically, takes up revenge tragedy to discuss it: his play might almost have been called *Antonio's Revenge Discussed*. He both accepts and examines the themes and techniques of the genre; he also plays his revenge tragedy to the hilt, but pauses occasionally to remark about that fact.

Marston, who was familiar with Shakespeare's plays, referred to them frequently throughout his career. *A Cynicke Satyre* (SV, 7) begins with the paraphrase: "A man, a man, a kingdome for a man." *Richard III* was a favorite play, and Richard's ability to play many roles like a fine actor made him a partner to Piero, Altofronto, Cocledemoy, and Hercules in their various ways. *Romeo and Juliet* was another play Marston could not get out of his mind.[8] Such is the strength and memorability of Shakespeare's characters that some of Marston's reflect them. Malevole smacks not only of Hamlet in his corrosive vein but also more than a little of the Thersites of *Troilus and Cressida*. Mamon, in *Jacke Drum's Entertainment*, occasionally recalls Shylock. The dull constabulary of *The Dutch Curtezan* comes from the same precinct station as Dogberry and Verges. In the outburst of satirical drama at the turn of the century, which both helped to start and fuel the quarrels which made up the War of the

Theaters, the combatant writers—Marston, Jonson, Dekker, Middleton, Shakespeare, and others—were well aware of what each other was doing. What Marston saw and heard in Shakespeare's excursions in this vein (parts of *Hamlet, Troilus and Cressida, All's Well That Ends Well,* and *Measure for Measure*) he had no occasion to forget or to ignore. Nonetheless, whatever such a character as Malevole may owe to others of his kind, he has, in the pattern of Marston's work, a perfectly adequate ancestry.[9]

In *Antonio's Revenge,* the balance is tantalizingly suggested between Marston as taker and giver. The play owes much to Kyd's *The Spanish Tragedy,* but the general theme and a variety of situations and effects are closely connected with *Hamlet.* The similarities between the two plays seem too close to be merely coincidental: "Poyson the father, butcher the son, & marrie the mother: ha? *Strotzo,* to bed: snort in securest sleepe" (1.74). There are hardly any close verbal parallels, however, between the two; and Marston was fond of using the language of plays that he took as his models or as his inspiration. Both plays may be based on an earlier version of the same story—a well-known one in any case, probably the mysterious *Ur-Hamlet.* The similarity in situations between the two plays is, however, obvious; but Marston treats his material very much in his own characteristic manner; and, though at times the reactions of, for example, Antonio and Hamlet, are semblable, the impression given by Marston is not one of a writer who is working directly from *Hamlet.*[10]

Janet Spens, in *Shakespeare's Relation to Tradition,* discusses the resemblances not only between *Antonio's Revenge* and *Hamlet* but between that play by Marston and *Macbeth.* Were Marston's play ever "acted in modern times, the likeness of its opening scenes (Act I., Scenes 1, 4, and 5) to those in *Macbeth,* Act II, could not have been overlooked. Piero's first entry, 'unbraced' and carrying in one hand a bloody dagger, in the other a torch, is very like the scene where Macbeth is on his way to the murder carrying a torch and a dagger. . . . Each has an attendant with him whom he dismisses, soliloquizing in something the same strain . . . we have stage situations which, if represented in dumb show, could not be distinguished. In each play a courtier enters announcing that he has found a Sovereign murdered. In both the only woman present faints, and is assisted out."[11] The comparisons need not be pursued, but the visual impact of some of Marston's scenes may have remained with Shakespeare.

Whether Jonson learned anything from his sometime partner, friend, and disciple is another matter, but he certainly had things to teach his apt though independent pupil. It is to Marston's credit that he was willing to be a pupil. Perhaps he began learning from Jonson by noting the dangers of arrogantly lecturing an audience on their shortcomings (it was a lesson that he had begun to study while still a verse satirist). The stage quarrel with Jonson must have forced Marston to study his rival's plays even more closely than he might naturally have done. He inevitably learned much about the art of comical satire from the exercise. From *The Malcontent* on, his plays were more tightly plotted, his language was more controlled, and his themes more sharply argued than they had been earlier. Obviously, not all this growing mastery of the stage can be attributed to Jonson, but the purge that master applied was clearly more extensive than appeared in *Poetaster* and affected more than the wilder excrescences of Marston's vocabulary.[12] Inevitably they fell to arguing again after *The Malcontent* had been dedicated to "his candid and heartfelt friend." But the last record of their "partnership" ought not to be Jonson's irascible criticisms and anecdotes that Drummond noted down in Scotland; rather it should be that, these sharp comments notwithstanding, a copy of Sheares's collection of Marston's plays was found to be in Jonson's library after his death in 1637. Marston wished to forget his theatrical past, but Jonson found it worthy of notice.

Clear debts to Marston are owed by Webster and Tourneur whose Italianate tragedies of revenge descend directly from *Antonio's Revenge* and *The Malcontent*.[13] Much in Webster harks back to Marston, whom he had possibly known in the Middle Temple and with whom he worked in adapting *The Malcontent* to the needs of the King's Men. Marston's sacrificing of structure to the needs of character exploitation and situation and his illustrating moments of tremendous impact at the expense of breaking the continuity of the narrative foreshadow Webster. The fusing of satire and tragedy especially appealed to Webster's imagination,[14] and Tourneur extended Marston's questioning of the ethical drive of revenge tragedy to its brilliant and cynical conclusion in *The Revenger's Tragedy* (indeed, in *The Atheist's Tragedy* he wrote what was essentially an anti–revenge tragedy).

The worlds of Marston and Fletcher are remote from each other, yet each is built upon shared foundations: "The rise of tragicomedy, satiric drama and the private theater are related phenomena . . . Fletcherian tragicomedy, though by no means the exclusive preserve of the private theater, clearly originated there and catered very successfully to its tastes."[15] Marston's interests and some characteristics of his drama are influences upon, rather than sources for, Fletcher. Marston's mingling of satirical comedy and tragedy—his reliance upon scenes of contrasting emotional mood fitted into the framework of a contrived plot (no matter how cavalier the contriving)—suggests a crude prototype of polished Fletcherian tragicomedy. Fletcher's scenes, of course, are smoothly ordered, and his emotional conflicts are handled with sophistication; he could mingle tragic and comic, but he was careful, unlike Marston, not to let them struggle confusedly together. In particular, he took great care not to disturb the atmosphere of his play; above all, he did not allow himself to poke fun at his grand-opera world.

Fletcher took his stage world seriously, for the artifice of the theater fascinated him as it did Marston. Fletcher, however, translated the drama into a sophisticated delight by the conjury of the stage. His was a brilliant manipulation of character and event that at one and the same time asked of the audience an acceptance of the trickery and a recognition of the cunning of the playwright and the actors who were entertaining them. This acceptance of a special relationship between author, actor, and audience traces part of its ancestry to Marston's brasher excitement in and exercise of the same relationship.

II *Marston's Qualities as Dramatist and Poet*

Whatever Marston's place among his contemporaries as receiver and giver, the individual quality of his plays must be judged. This quality may be measured in terms of language, of theme and its argument, and of theatrical effect and dramatic propriety. In regard to his style, Marston tells the reader of *The Malcontent:* "I am an ill Oratour; and in truth, use to indite more honestly than eloquently, for it is my custome to speake as I thinke, and write as I speake" (1.139). He spoke as he thought, even when he thought rather incoherently or confusedly. One gathers that he also wrote as he spoke, for his satires are furious monologues that ask to be read aloud rather than silently, and the voice heard in them is that which easily cut through the cry of the other satirists in the 1590s and that announced Marston very definitely to his fellows. His own ear for the spoken word served him well, and he commanded a range of styles from the impressive nobility of Andrugio to the light rattle of the idle

courtiers, from the harsh power of Malevole to the finely balanced
mockery of much of *The Fawne*. His plays are crowded with people
who speak naturally, and they are as liable to rise to a flow of
passionate exhortation as to fall to a hesitant nervousness. During
Marston's age, the art of the "oratour" was formal, mannered,
controlled—the delivery of set pieces. Neither Marston nor his
characters used such methods, not even Andrugio at his most
eloquent. Marston's characters speak as they think; and they break
away, therefore, from the speech patterns of earlier tragedy and
comedy. This observation does not indicate, however, that the stress
of the moment does not affect their language and style as they express
their twisting thoughts and half-thoughts in language that is familiar
but image-packed. The model is the speaker of the verse satires who
is driven by his questing and questioning mind; for he leaps from
topic to topic, from point to point, before one is fully developed or
made: his is a rushing, allusive, poetically charged speech.

Marston's plays often read more stiffly and awkwardly than they
sound, for the speeches lose some of their strangeness when they are
heard. Marston, more than any of his contemporaries, was aware of
how much of his art might elude the printed word: "If any shall
wonder why I print a Comedie, whose life rests much in the Actors
voice, Let such know, that it cannot avoid publishing: let it therefore
stand with good excuse, that I have been my owne setter out"
(2.143). He took care over his plays; and, if they had to be printed, he
took care over their printing.[16]

Marston's style is intimately bound up with his presentation of an
uneasily questioning, insecure, dangerously deceptive world.
Marston's vision of society was by its nature difficult to shape
artistically, and his problems were worsened because his own
understanding of it was not complete. The solutions and solace he was
eventually to find in the church and its ministry were only to be
reached after ten years of arduous struggle as a writer. When he
turned to playwriting he was still in the early stages of his analysis of
society, for he was, after all, just thirty-three when he was ordained.
Inevitably, he pursued his work in a Christian framework, but that
did not preclude him from testing the stoic philosophies of Seneca
and Epictetus, the enlightened skepticism of Montaigne, or more
orthodox Christian tenets. In this pursuit, he reflects one of the
central spiritual and philosophical occupations of his era. He urges his
views on society's ills and the cures they demanded in his satires
turbulently and bewilderingly; and he conducted the trials on the

stage, especially in his first plays, with hardly more decorum. Conflicting opinions were heard, voices were often raised raucously, laughter was heard in court, not all of which was perhaps anticipated, but the trial itself never became a mockery.

Marston's willingness to talk about acting and dramatic genres before and during his plays is a part not only of his concern about theatricality, but of his views of and preoccupation with the problems of life and thought itself. Probing the appearance of things at large meant, in the theater, investigating the accepted genres and modes of representing and imitating life. Marston accepts nothing at face value; he has an overmastering urge to demonstrate that confusion and paradox inhere in life, that simple dichotomies of good and bad are deceptive, that the sight of sin does not automatically augment the hatred of vice, that innocence is no shield for a moralist. His court of judgment deals with issues that cannot be decided by a neat "guilty" or "not guilty"; for complexity, uncertainty, and lack of stability deny simple solutions. Revenge is not merely an eye for an eye, a tooth for a tooth; it is not the pursuit of the wicked by implacable men with untarnished noble aspirations. Marston's revengers are not single-minded pursuers of a victim, from the simple view that one is right and the other wrong. Andrugio, Feliche, and Antonio debate not how they should achieve their purpose, but what it is they ought to do—and whether they should do anything.[17] Old-fashioned pursuit of revenge leads only to the bloody and pointless killing of children such as Julio, and, as Duke Pietro discovers, to know that a wife has been unfaithful does not automatically fill one with a holy crusading joy to punish her. Pietro's reaction is Othello's: "But yet the pitty of it, *Iago*; oh *Iago*, the pitty of it *Iago*" (4.1.2580). Marston's anger is not that of a coarse man but of a sensitive one; but he neither parades his sensitivity nor cheapens it into sentimentality. His candid expression of it sustains his best work and results in his most moving scenes.

Naked ambition and revenge are insufficient for tragedy in Marston, and conventional depictions of love do not make a comedy in his theater. One can no more trust that vice will be repulsive on sight than that love will come at first sight, unproblematically, and lead cheerfully to the easy comfort of "they all lived happily ever after." The strength of affection between Altofronto and Maria, Beatrice and Freevill, Tysefew and Crispinella, and Sophonisba and Massinissa cannot be doubted; but it is not presented in any conventional romantic way. This fact recognized, it must be admitted that the force of convention, the usually accepted demands of the genres, and the thrust of Marston's arguments are not always satisfactorily weighted against one another. To entertain doubts is not always to settle them adequately or dramatically, and the ending of *Antonio's Revenge* is inconclusive because Marston himself had perhaps reached no conclusions firm enough to be mirrored in a convincing ending. Marston was right, however, to tease at the meaning of the genres, for they do not completely contain his arguments. As Madeleine Doran has observed, "The difficulty with these plays is that the problems are realistically viewed, the endings are not. Fortuitous solutions do not usually come to moral problems."[18] But a contrived ending does not necessarily invalidate the endeavor of art that led to it.

Marston takes stock characters, puts them into familiar situations, and then surprises expectation by having them behave "out of character" so that it is hard to know them for what they at first were thought to be. Disguise is the center of Marston's art: actors assume a character for a play, and then the character in that play adopts other disguises. Villains and heroes, earnest men and comedians, men and women, are all of them likely to be different persons at different times, shifting their character as easily as they shift clothes.

This device is, of course, common in the Elizabethan theater; but Marston's particular handling of it claims attention. The fact that all his actors were often boys did not make his plays as parodic as some critics believe, but it was a fact of theatrical life for Marston which he proceeded to turn to his advantage. Boys were, after all, actors as were men; and the pretense of the stage world was his image of the real world's deceptiveness. Because he read life as a mixture of comedy and tragedy further confused by the presence of satire, he made his plays reflect those generic confrontations and mixtures. Marston had used such juxtapositions in his satires—not always successfully—and had discovered that, where they had worked in the satires, they emerged on the stage with greatly enhanced impact as a disturbingly accurate comment on man's behavior.

By trial and error, however, Marston learned that the seemingly random collisions and abrupt changes of gear only worked artistically when deliberation and care justified the word "seemingly." The danger of practicing the "absurd" method is that, with only the slightest miscalculation, the end result is merely stupid or pointless. To argue that there are conflicts which are accidental, as it were, and conflicts which are deliberate is not, of course, to assert that it is a simple matter to distinguish which is which when they occur. To expect to be able to do so with any degree of precision is to expect too much. To recognize the principle and to suggest some applications of it is a sanguine enough hope.

Adaptation of satire to the stage occupied stronger and better minds than Marston's at the turn of the sixteenth century, such as those of Jonson and Shakespeare; but none brought more zest and excitement or more natural theatrical gifts to the task than he did. More than many of his fellow playwrights, Marston was directly and unabashedly fascinated by the art of the theater: its essential artifice, its juggling with illusion and reality, its pretense and actuality; the interplay between the author, the actor and his role, and the audience; the contrasting patterns of sound and vision provided by the spectacle of the stage, the counterpoint of different voices, the movement of people, the fusing of words, action, music, and other sounds. He delighted in all of these aspects and explored them brilliantly and, at times, recklessly. He was a theatrical man in the baser sense of the word, for he was undeniably a posturing extravagant.

More importantly, Marston was a theatrical man in the richer sense of the word, one whose natural gifts found exciting and spontaneous expression on the stage. He possessed prodigious gifts no matter how much he sometimes abused them. "It is hard to find another instance of a man thus suffered to pass on to the hands of masters the vision he himself could not express, transmitting to them images, phrases, situations which just fail in his hands of becoming poetry and with them become inevitable and immortal. Truly, as the witch said to Banquo, 'Thou shalt get kings though thou be none,' and that in itself is no slight boon."[19] Possibly Marston might be called the playwright's playwright. This is a lesser thing than being the dramatist's dramatist, but it was an achievement during the richest period of England's stage history.

Notes and References

Preface

1. A. C. Swinburne, *The Age of Shakespeare* (London, 1908), pp. 110–11.
2. The views of these critics are found in T. S. Eliot, "John Marston," *Elizabethan Essays* (London, 1934), pp. 177–95; Alfred Harbage, *Shakespeare and the Rival Traditions* (New York, 1952), passim; Robert Ornstein, *The Moral Vision of Jacobean Tragedy* (Madison, Wis., 1960), pp. 151–63; Samuel Schoenbaum, "The Precarious Balance of John Marston," *Publications of the Modern Language Association*, LXVII (1952), pp. 1069–78.

Chapter One

1. David G. O'Neill, "The Commencement of Marston's Career as a Dramatist," *Review of English Studies*, XXII (1971), pp. 442–45.
2. This figure is taken from Philip J. Finkelpearl, *John Marston of the Middle Temple: An Elizabethan Dramatist in his Social Setting* (Cambridge, Mass., 1969), the first six chapters of which ("The Milieu of the Inns of Court") provide the best survey of its intellectual activity in the late sixteenth century.
3. *Ibid.*, p. 69.
4. There is also the unnamed play for which Henslowe prepaid Marston "the new poete" forty shillings. Marston may have been new to playwriting or merely new to Henslowe: it cannot be said whether this was the only play on which he tried his apprentice hand. The full entry in *Henslowe's Diary*, ed. R. A. Foakes and R. T. Rickert (Cambridge, 1961), p. 124 is: "Lent unto wm Borne the 28 of Septmb, 1599 to Lent unto mr maxton the new poete mr mastone in earneste of a Boocke called the some of xxxxs." " 'Mr mastone' is interlined with caret. Greg regards this as a modern forgery; we think it was inserted by Henslowe" (editors' note, p. 124). The space left for the play's name was never filled in.
5. From Marston's prefatory note "To the generall reader" (2.5). In the quarto, 1606, the text reads "English black-verse" which is corrected to "blank-verse" in the 1633 collection. It is probably too much to read the original as Marston's intention.
6. Jonson's comment on the marriage was: "Marston wrott his Father-in-lawes preachings & his Father-in-Law his Commedies" (Her-

160

ford & Simpson, I, 138). Wilkes, I imagine, is being made to serve as playwright in order to let Jonson fire a shot at Marston's didacticism which was at times zealously direct; Jonson had probably experienced it personally!

7. This affair is fully dealt with by E. K. Chambers in *The Elizabethan Stage* (Oxford, 1923, repr. with corrections 1951), II, 53–55 and III, 257–58. The quotation is from a letter to Lord Salisbury from Sir Thomas Luke, a clerk of the signet attending James and reporting that James, "though he had signified his mynde to your lo, by my lo. of Mountgommery yet I should repeate it again, That his G. had vowed they should never play more. . ." Quoted on pp. 53–55.

8. See Finkelpearl, *op. cit.,* pp. 220–27.

Chapter Three

1. Joseph Hall, *Characters of Vertues and Vices: in two Bookes,* ed. Rudolph Kirk (New Brunswick, N. J., 1948), pp. 178–79. Taken from "The Second Booke. Characterismes of Vices: of the Male-content."

2. See Theodore Spencer, "The Elizabethan Malcontent," in *Joseph Quincy Adams Memorial Studies* (Washington, 1948), pp. 523–35.

3. Theodore Spencer, *Shakespeare and the Nature of Man* (New York, 1949), p. 46.

4. *Ibid.,* p. 46.

5. Alvin Kernan, *The Cankered Muse* (New Haven, 1959), p. 55.

6. *Ibid.,* p. 135.

7. Despite the rich labor of Arnold Davenport in the notes to his edition of Marston's poems, every allusion in the satires has not been explained. The satires are not in general effect as puzzling or as irritating as they have often been made out to be. Marston had his own comment on this matter in words to the judicial perusers of his satires: "*Chaucer* is harde even to our understandings: who knowes not the reason? howe much more those old Satyres which expresse themselves in termes, that breathed not long even in their daies. But had we then lived, the understanding of them had been nothing hard" (23–28). The "nothing hard" is a piece of Marstonian special pleading, but the general tenor of his remarks is just.

8. Arnold Davenport, *The Poems of John Marston* (Liverpool, 1961), p. 338.

Chapter Four

1. *Francis Meres's Treatise "Poetrie,"* ed. Don Cameron Allen (Urbana, Ill., 1933), p. 69b, lines 12–20.

2. Sir Walter Raleigh, *The Historie of the World* (London, 1666), 2nd edition. Preface D4v.

3. Marston was well known for his red hair and short legs. Jonson twitted him for them in *Poetaster*, but the edge of the jest was turned away because Marston himself frequently alluded to these features with easy good humor: "But in good veritie la, he is as proper a gentleman in reversion as: and indeede, as fine a man as may be, having a red beard and a pair of warpt legges" (*Malcontent*, 1.209). See *Antonio and Mellida*, 1.36; *What You Will*, 2.274–75. A reference to red hair and little legs in *Lust's Dominion* is used by Gustav Cross as one of his arguments for attributing the play to Marston.

4. The device is not unusual in Elizabethan drama and is found, indeed, in *Eastward Hoe* when Security, the usurer, is unwittingly the pander for his own wife. Finkelpearl, *op. cit.*, p. 137; see also 137–39, 163–64, which finds the identification of Brabant, Sr. with Jonson "an utterly groundless guess," largely because he looks for that consistency of portraiture which I suggest is not always needed.

5. R. A. Small, *The Stage Quarrel Between Ben Jonson and the So-called Poetasters* (Breslau, 1899), p. 132.

Chapter Five

1. Finkelpearl, *op. cit.*, pp. 122–23.

2. Review of A. J. Axelrad, *Un Malcontent Élisabéthain John Marston* in *Etudes Anglaises*, VIII (1955), p. 341.

3. Coventry Patmore's review of Bullen's edition of Marston's *Works* originally published in the *St. James Gazette*, May 28, 1887, reprinted in his *Courage in Politics* (London, 1921), pp. 51–54.

4. See bibliography for Cross's series of articles in *Notes and Queries*. Muriel Bradbrook, *Themes and Conventions of Elizabethan Tragedy* (London, 1935), p. 83, comments on Shakespeare's coining of words as a parallel case to Marston.

5. G. K. Hunter, preface to *Antonio and Mellida*, Regents Renaissance Drama Series (Lincoln, Neb., 1965), p. xviii. R. A. Foakes discusses *Antonio and Mellida* using this quotation from Hunter as a springboard to some contrary opinions about the play in *Shakespeare the Dark Comedies to the Last Plays: from Satire to Celebration* (London, 1971), pp. 39–43. His conclusion is: "If he [Marston] had serious ethical aims, then I think in this play they dissolve in the comedy; but however that may be, *Antonio and Mellida* is a delightful and successful play in another sense, in finding a new way of exploiting satire" (43).

6. G. K. Hunter, "*Henry IV* and the Elizabethan Two-Part Play," *Review of English Studies*, XIX (1954), pp. 236–48. There are further remarks in the introduction to his edition of *Antonio's Revenge*. Regents Renaissance Drama Series (Lincoln, Neb., 1965), pp. ix–xii.

7. This startling entry is reminiscent—probably deliberately so—of

Hieronimo's entry with a dagger in one hand and a rope in the other to commit suicide in *The Spanish Tragedy*. The several links that exist between Marston's plays and Kyd's are conveniently gathered together and discussed by R. A. Foakes, *op. cit.*, pp. 65–70.

8. Fredson Bowers, *Elizabethan Revenge Tragedy 1587–1642* (Princeton, 1940), p. 123.

9. Rosamond Gilder, "The Hamlet Tradition—Some Notes on Costume, Scenery, and Stage Business," *John Gielgud's Hamlet* (New York, 1937), taken from *Interpreting Hamlet*, ed. Russell E. Leavenworth (San Francisco, 1960), pp. 160–61.

10. *Samuel Johnson on Shakespeare*, ed. W. K. Wimsatt, Jr. (New York, 1960), p. 39. The phrase comes from Johnson's discussion of the unities in his Preface to "The Plays of William Shakespeare" (1765).

11. *The Malcontent*, ed. Martin Wine, Regents Renaissance Drama Series, (Lincoln, Neb., 1965), p. xvii.

12. *Antonio and Mellida*, ed. G. K. Hunter (Lincoln, Neb., 1965), pp. xiv–xv.

13. *Ibid.*, p. xvi.

14. *Ibid.*, p. xix.

15. Martin Esslin, *The Theatre of the Absurd*, rev. & enlarged ed. (London, 1968), p. 10.

16. Clifford Leech examines qualities of Absurdism in literature during the last 350 years in "When Writing Becomes Absurd," *Colorado Quarterly*, XIII (1964), pp. 6–24. See also R. W. Ingram, *"Gammer Gurton's Needle:* Comedy not Quite of the Lowest Order," *Studies in English Literature*, VII (1967), pp. 258–68.

17. *Antonio's Revenge* is both more serious and more flamboyant than *Antonio and Mellida* and so more susceptible to parody. The mockery must not be overemphasized, however. The Induction to *Antonio and Mellida* was never a direct prelude to *Antonio's Revenge*. The boy's concern about acting the part of Piero and his jaunty assumption of confidence in the role belongs essentially to another play as far as the audience watching *Antonio's Revenge* is concerned. The roles are related but the connection between actor and his part is tested differently in the two plays. G. K. Hunter has some relevant remarks on parody in the introduction to his edition of *Antonio and Mellida*, (Lincoln, Neb., 1965), pp. xvi–xvii. See also R. A. Foakes, *op. cit.*, pp. 38–43.

18. R. A. Foakes, "Shakespeare's Later Tragedies", *Shakespeare 1564–1964*, ed. E. A. Bloom (Providence, 1964), p. 95.

Chapter Six

1. It has usually been thought that the play stolen by the Boys was *I Jeronimo* (1600–1604?). However, it is possible that it was the theft of the

more popular *Spanish Tragedy* that inspired the King's Men to retaliate so boldly. See G. K. Hunter's footnote to line 78 of the Induction in his edition of *The Malcontent* (Revels Plays, 1975).

2. All of the additions occur in the first and last acts where adjustments can usually best be made. Ten additional passages exist; seven are light comedy concerned with Bilioso and Passarello (the latter character was specially created for the King's Men); three add importantly to Malevole's role. No addition stands out awkwardly; indeed, without the two versions to compare, it would be impossible accurately to point to the extra lines. Although contributing to atmosphere and comedy, the new material does slow the action a little at times.

3. *The Malcontent,* ed. Bernard Harris, The New Mermaids (London, 1967), p. xvi.

4. These words are from the program notes by Jonathan Miller for his production of the play at Nottingham in 1968. As testimony from an experienced professional director, Miller's fuller comment is worth stating: "Confronted by a text that has not been performed since it was first written one can usually understand why. In the case of *The Malcontent* though it's hard to understand why it has taken so long. The piece almost plays itself and seems to insist on being played, watched and enjoyed. The plot is simple, the argument clear. Only the texture is rich. In fact the whole surface of the play glistens with comic invention; darkened throughout by a rich thrilling pessimism. The piece echoes a number of Shakespearean themes and one is reminded again and again of *The Tempest, Measure for Measure* and *Hamlet.*"

5. *Antonio's Revenge,* ed. G. K. Hunter (Lincoln, Neb., 1965), p. xvii.

Chapter Seven

1. Gustav Cross, "Marston, Montaigne, and Morality: *The Dutch Courtesan* Reconsidered," *English Literary History,* XXVII (1960), p. 33.

2. M. C. Bradbrook, *The Growth and Structure of Elizabethan Comedy* (London, 1961), p. 45.

3. H. G. Matthews' review of 1964 production of *The Dutch Courtesan* in *Theatre World,* LX (August, 1964), p. 31. A very condescending criticism that leaves opaque what is meant by a popular audience of early Jacobean days: private or public theater audience? the same audience that gathered for Shakespeare? The whole review took what might be called an early-Malheureux tone. See also p. 3 of introduction to Peter Davison's edition of this play.

4. Cyrus Hoy, *The Hyacinth Room* (London, 1964), p. 198. This is taken from Chapter VII, "Reason Overthrown," which is an excellent discussion of drama dealing with the conflict of the rational and man's pride in reason and the ways in which his physical nature—especially if abused or

repressed—undermines that reason. *The Dutch Courtesan* is treated at length. Comedy, Hoy argues, is particularly adept at containing this conflict. "Thus the saturnalian quality of so much of comic incident, wherein rational restraints are suspended as irrational urge runs riot, and the sober intellect looks on helplessly at the folly it is powerless to curb" (p. 200). It is Marston's gift to qualify this behavior a little in his main plot—Malheureux's urge runs not quite riot; it does not swamp his loyalty to Freevill, for instance; and no more is Freevill helpless to curb his friend. The riotous comedy generated by the whole problem, however, runs its course in much freer manner in the antic course run by Cocledemoy. In this sense, Marston controls his main plot yet infuses his comedy as a whole with the joy of "the irrational urge run wild."

5. Hoy, *op. cit.*, p. 196. These comments were quoted in the program notes to the National Theatre production of the play by William Gaskell and Piers Haggard in London and Chichester, 1964. Joan Littlewood had earlier produced the play in Theatre Workshop in London in 1958. Both productions were loudly enjoyed by their audiences who very obviously found much to delight them in the play.

Joan Littlewood's program notes summed up Marston's dramatic power as follows: "There are no lay figures, no heroes, no villains and no types to be found in most of Marston's work. Above all, there are real women . . . he was the only dramatist of the Golden Age of the English Theatre who could write as real women think." William Gaskell comments on the play in an interview with Frank Cox recorded in *Plays and Players*, XI (July, 1964), p. 10.

The two kinds of critical reaction to Marston may be exampled easily from reviews of this production. In *Theatre World*, LX (August, 1964), H. G. M. said of the play: "It reflects a popular audience of early Jacobean days and offers crude entertainment for crude minds." The affairs of Cocledemoy were particularly distasteful to the same stern moralist: "The entirely separate subplot showed various practical jokes amounting to persecution played upon Master Mulligrub. . . . If one took the sufferer's point of view, it would, of course, mar enjoyment, but Cocledemoy seemed to be actuated by nothing but pure mischief" (31).

Not surprisingly, the advertisements chose to quote other critics; inside the front cover of the same issue of *Theatre World*, one might read that: "Half a dozen plots . . . whirl about to considerable comic effect making their points with robust and vulgar wit . . . and plenty of farcical situations,"— Bernard Levin, *Daily Mail*. "Roguish, bawdy, and beyond a censor's reach," wrote Herbert Kretzmer, *Daily Express;* "A racy equivalent of our own domestic comedy . . . frank, ribald and uninhibited," said Milton Shulman, *Evening Standard*.

6. M. C. Bradbrook, *op. cit.*, p. 152.

7. No production I have ever seen was able to do much for Bertram; he is not popular either with audiences or with actors. He wins the heroine at the

end but not very enthusiastically; rather, she persists in winning him. Marston avoids this awkwardness by effectively removing Malheureux from true romantic ardor and by using Freevill as the "romantic hero."

Chapter Eight

1. Finkelpearl, *op. cit.*, pp. 227–29, but especially his article, "The Use of the Middle Temple's Christmas Revels in Marston's *The Fawne,*" *Studies in Philology,* XLIV (1967), pp. 199–209.

Chapter Nine

1. Anthony Caputi, *John Marston, Satirist* (Ithaca, N. Y., 1961), p. 243.
2. Lehman Engel, *Words with Music* (New York, 1972), p. 10. Although music has, of course, not been abandoned by the theater, it might be said that the film has largely taken over and further developed the traditional and received customs of music in the theater.

Chapter Ten

1. Sheares's dedicatory letter is at pains to deny any obscenity or offensiveness in the plays, so much so that it suggests Marston's notoriety was not forgotten in 1633. Sheares makes matters worse by denying the old charges and then adding a rider that if they were true the author's youth was sufficient excuse. Whether the charges were true or not, the fact that Sheares aired them again and dealt with them so clumsily must have irritated Marston.
2. Gerald E. Bentley, *The Jacobean and Caroline Stage* (Oxford, 1941–56), I, 123. Bentley, *op. cit.*, II, 690, quotes Edmund Gayton's *Pleasant Notes upon Don Quixote* (1654): "yet men come not to study at a Play-house, but love such expressions and passages, which with ease insinuate themselves into their capacities . . . to them bring *Jack Drum's Entertainment, Greens tu quoque,* the *Devill of Edmunton* . . ." Marston's title is a proverbial phrase, but the context here suggests that it is the play that is a byword for a particular kind of play.
3. Excluding such publications as Sir William Alexander's *The Monarchicke Tragedies* which were closet dramas, the list of collected editions runs:
1616: Ben Jonson, *The Works.*
1621: Thomas Middleton, *Honorable Entertainments* (strictly speaking, by-blows from his major theatrical work).
1623: Samuel Daniel, *The Works.*
       William Shakespeare, *Commedies, Histories* & *Tragedies.*
1632: Johy Lyly, *Sixe Court Comedies.*
4. Wood, *Plays of Marston,* III, xxiii.

5. Brian Gibbons, *Jacobean City Comedy* (London, 1968), p. 28. For a much sterner view of this procedure, see David Frost, *The School of Shakespeare* (Cambridge, 1968). Frost frequently looks on the borrowing by members of the school—Middleton, Massinger, Webster, Ford, Marston, Beaumont, and Fletcher—as reprehensible and as morally bad. Shakespeare is presented as the source of most that is good in Elizabethan drama. Marston is marked as a notorious borrower, but some allowance is made for his idiosyncratic use of what he borrowed: "Confident in a collection of borrowed episodes and characters, Marston might use, elaborate and relate them in new ways" (184). Of course, Marston is a borrower, but not so indigent a one as Frost suggests.

6. A convenient survey of Marston's Classical knowledge, as it is revealed in the poems, is given by Davenport, *The Poems*, pp. 28–30. G. K. Hunter, "Seneca and the Elizabethans: A Case Study in 'Influence'," *Shakespeare Survey*, XX (1967), pp. 17–26, is the best treatment of this important topic.

7. Jean Fuzier, "Carrière et Popularité de la 'Tragédie Espagnole' en Angleterre," *Dramaturgie et Société*, ed. J. Jaquot (Paris, 1968), II, 589–606. Claude Dudrap, "La 'Tragedie Espagnole' face à la critique Elisabéthaine et Jacobéene," *ibid.*, II, 607–31. The fifty-nine plays referring to *The Spanish Tragedy* are listed in an appendix to this article.

8. There are parodies of *Richard III* (the queens' lament 2.2, 4.4) in *Antonio's Revenge* (1.92), and of *Romeo and Juliet* (2.2) in *Jacke Drum's Entertainment* (3.200–201). Stilling notes a series of connections, some of them comical, between *Romeo and Juliet* and *Antonio and Mellida* (*Love and Death in Renaissance Tragedy*, 83–89 *passim*).

9. B. Ifor Evans, *A Short History of English Drama* (Harmondsworth, 1948) p. 78. Commenting about Marston, Evans mentions, apropos of *Hamlet* and Marston: "It is of interest that Shakespeare went out of his way in *Hamlet* to discuss the controversy of the boy-players and the adult-players, and this was a matter in which Marston was deeply involved. In verse and language Marston belongs to the earlier Elizabethan tradition, and seems ever in danger of straining the verse too far. It may be that Shakespeare had some such thoughts in mind in his comments on verse in *Hamlet* in the player's speech." A. J. Axelrad, *Un Malcontent Elizabéthain: John Marston (1576–1634)*, (Paris, 1955), p. 315, suggests a borrowing by Shakespeare—in *Macbeth*—from *Sophonisba*, of a distinctive image.

10. Frost, *op. cit.*, devotes a chapter to "The Impact of *Hamlet* on the Revenge Tradition" (pp. 167–208) and supports his arguments for Shakespeare's primacy in all respects in an appendix (pp. 276–79). G. K. Hunter's view is found in the preface to his edition of *Antonio's Revenge*, pp. xviii–xxi. McGinn's survey of *Hamlet's* influence is very full but anxiously overargued and weighty with unconvincing parallels. See also B. Ifor Evans, *op. cit.*, p. 78.

11. Janet Spens, *Shakespeare's Relation to Tradition* (Oxford, 1916), pp. 82–83, 85.

12. He at least satisfied Jonson that he had corrected more than vocabulary troubles; for the two of them, with Chapman, joined to write a year or two later, *Eastward Hoe*.

13. For Webster's debts to Marston, see especially Travis Bogard, *The Tragic Satire of John Webster* (Berkeley, 1955), *passim*.

14. Elizabeth M. Brennan, " 'An Understanding Auditory': An Audience for John Webster," in *John Webster*, Mermaid Critical Commentaries, ed. Brian Morris (London, 1970), pp. 3–19, comments interestingly on some links between Marston and Webster (especially pp. 9–13, concerning *The White Devil*).

15. Arthur C. Kirsch, *Jacobean Dramatic Perspectives* (Charlottesville, 1972), p. 5, good discussion of the problems of tragicomedy in the Jacobean theater. See also J. R. Mulryne, "Webster and the Uses of Tragicomedy," in *John Webster*, ed. Morris, pp. 131–56. The relationship of Marston's work to late Shakespeare and to Fletcherian tragicomedy is further examined by Kirsch in "Cymbeline and Coterie Dramaturgy", *English Literary History* 34 (1967), pp. 285–306.

16. This may explain Sheares's apology that Marston had not himself been able to check the proofs of the 1633 volume. It may even have added to Marston's ire that, if his plays were to be reissued, he had not been given chance to check them in any way.

17. Robert Ornstein, *The Moral Vision of Jacobean Tragedy* (Madison, 1960), p. 156, comments: "The intrusion of Stoic philosophy in the Revenge, for example, is strictly speaking fraudulent. It adds a 'philosophical' complication that has no organic purpose in Marston's fable. Yet the pitting of Senecan philosophy against Senecan revenge motivation is in itself an inspired innovation which later dramatists (e.g. Chapman and Tourneur) make dramatically and morally significant." This is true if one agrees that Marston is (or ought to be) concerned only with his fable and not with some ramifications of it. It may be that Marston debates the revenge ethic rather than the characters in his play, but I believe his intent is for the debate—for the 'intrusion'—to be part of the fable's progress.

18. Madeleine Doran, *Endeavors of Art* (Madison, 1954), p. 367. The same judgment can be applied to Shakespeare's problem comedies, and the issue is evaded, not solved, when John Barton ends a production of *Measure for Measure* with Isabella alone on the stage, clearly unwilling and refusing to marry the Duke.

19. Una Ellis-Fermor, *The Jacobean Drama*, 4th ed. (London, 1958), p. 97.

Selected Bibliography

PRIMARY SOURCES

1. Collected Editions

The Works of John Marston. Edited, with an introduction, by A. H. Bullen. 3 vols. London: John C. Nimmo, 1887. The sixty-page introduction surveys Marston's life; makes sparing and generally not very enthusiastic commentary upon his work.

The Plays of John Marston. Edited by H. Harvey Wood. 3 vols. Edinburgh: Oliver and Boyd, 1934–1939. The only complete edition of the plays (it includes *The Insatiate Countess* and *Eastward Hoe*), old spelling. The plays have separate introductions; there is a brief life of Marston in volume I and an excellent essay on "Marston as a Dramatic Author" in volume III.

The Poems of John Marston. Edited, with introduction and commentary, by Arnold Davenport. Liverpool: Liverpool University Press, 1961. The standard edition; copiously annotated; excellent introductory essay.

2. Some Editions of Single Works

Antonio and Mellida. Edited by George K. Hunter. Lincoln: University of Nebraska Press, 1965. Regents Renaissance Drama Series. Hunter's introductions to this and to *Antonio's Revenge* are the best criticism of Marston since Spencer.

Antonio's Revenge. Edited by George K. Hunter. Lincoln: University of Nebraska Press, 1965. Regents Renaissance Drama Series.

The Malcontent. Edited by Martin Wine. Lincoln: University of Nebraska Press, 1965. Regents Renaissance Drama Series. Edited by Bernard Harris. London: Ernest Benn, 1967. The New Mermaids. Edited by George K. Hunter. London: Methuen, 1975. The Revels Plays.

The Dutch Courtesan. Edited by Martin Wine. Lincoln: University of Nebraska Press, 1965. Regents Renaissance Drama Series. Edited by Peter Davison. Berkeley and Los Angeles: University of California Press, 1968. The Fountainwell Drama Texts. This is an old spelling edition.

The Fawn. Edited by Gerald A. Smith. Lincoln: University of Nebraska Press, 1964. Regents Renaissance Drama Series.

3. Editions of Works by Marston's Contemporaries

BRETON, NICHOLAS. *No Whippinge*. Liverpool: Liverpool University Press, 1951. In *The Whipper Pamphlets (1601)* Pt. II. Ed. Arnold Davenport.

GUILPIN, EVERARD. *Skialetheia*, 1598. Ed., G. B. Harrison. Oxford: Oxford University Press, 1931.

————. *The Whipper of the Satyre his Penaunce*, in *The Whipper Pamphlets (1601)*, Pt. II. Ed., Arnold Davenport. Liverpool: Liverpool University Press, 1951.

HALL, JOSEPH. *The Collected Poems of Joseph Hall*. Ed., Arnold Davenport. Liverpool: Liverpool University Press, 1949.

JONSON, BEN. *The Works of Ben Jonson*. Ed., C. H. Herford, Percy & Evelyn Simpson. 11 vols. Oxford: Oxford University Press, 1925–52.

MANNINGHAM, JOHN. *The Diary of John Manningham of the Middle Temple 1602–1603*. Newly edited in complete and unexpurgated form from the original manuscript in the British Museum, with introduction and notes, by Robert Parker Sorlien. Hanover, N. H.: University Press of New England, 1976.

SHAKESPEARE, WILLIAM. *The First Folio of Shakespeare*. The Norton Facsimile. Prepared by Charlton Hinman. New York: Norton, 1968.

WEEVER, JOHN. *Faunus and Melliflora (1600)*. Ed., Arnold Davenport. Liverpool: Liverpool University Press, 1948.

————. *The Whipping of the Satyre* in *The Whipper Pamphlets (1601)* Pt. I. Ed., Arnold Davenport. Liverpool: Liverpool University Press, 1951.

ANONYMOUS. *The Three Parnassus Plays* (1598–1601). Ed., J. B. Leishman. London: 1949. Has a good lengthy introduction with some particular study of Marston, Hall, and the War of the Theatres (pp. 82–92)

SECONDARY SOURCES

ANONYMOUS. "Theatre of Cruelty in the Middle Temple: the Plays of John Marston," *Times Literary Supplement* (Feb 5, 1971), 155–57. Favorable review of Finkelpearl's book (q.v.) which is fine short essay primarily concerned with the two parts of *Antonio and Mellida*.

AGGELER, GEOFFREY D. "Stoicism and Revenge in Marston," *English Studies*, LI (1970), 1–10. Suggests Marston's steady interest in ethical problems presented to an adherent of Stoic moral philosophy, drawing on moral essays of Seneca, Epictetus, and Plutarch. Examples from the two parts of *Antonio and Mellida* and *The Malcontent*.

ALDEN, R. M. *The Rise of Formal Satire in England under Classical Influence*. Pennsylvania University Series in Philology, Literature and Archaeology, Vol. VII, No. 2. Philadelphia: University of Pennsylvania Press, 1899. Useful survey; very critical of Marston.

AXELRAD, A. JOSE. *Un Malcontent Elizabéthain: John Marston (1576–1634).*
Paris, Didier 1955. Sound, comprehensive study.

BABB, LAWRENCE. *The Elizabethan Malady: A Study of Melancholia in English
Literature from 1580 to 1642.* East Lansing: Michigan State College
Press, 1951. Standard work: Chapter 4, "The Malcontent Types."

BERGSON, ALLEN. "Dramatic Style as Parody in Marston's *Antonio and
Mellida,*" *Studies in English Literature,* XI (1971), 307–25. The unlikely
reformations of romantic comedy in the first part are answered by
the bloody excesses of revenge tragedy in the second part.

————. "The Ironic Tragedy of Marston and Chapman: Notes on the
Jacobean Tragic Form," *Journal of English and Germanic Philology,*
LXIX (1970), 613–30. Compares the two parts of *Antonio and Mellida*
and Chapman's *Bussy D'Ambois* and the *Conspiracy and Tragedy of
Byron* as concerned with "disguise, the false appearances that cover
both the personality and the world, as well as about the truths they
are used to conceal."

BERLAND, ELLEN. "The Function of Irony in Marston's *Antonio and
Mellida,*" *Studies in Philology,* LXVI (1969), 739–55. The play is a
parody of romantic comedy meant to amuse, not to edify.

BOWERS, FREDSON. *Elizabethan Revenge Tragedy 1587–1642.* Princeton:
Princeton University Press, 1940. Standard survey.

BRETTLE, R.E. "Bibliographical notes on some Marston Quartos and early
collected editions" *Library,* VIII, 4th series (1927–28), 336–48.

————. "Everard Guilpin and John Marston (1576–1634)" *Review of
English Studies,* XVI (1965), 396–99. Proves the two satirists related
by marriage.

————. "John Marston, Dramatist at Oxford," *ibid.,* III (1927), 398–405.

————. "John Marston, Dramatist, Some New Facts about His Life,"
Modern Language Review, XXII (1927), 7–14.

————. "Marston Born in Oxfordshire," *ibid.* XXII (1927), 317–19.

————. "Notes on John Marston," *Review of English Studies,* XIII (1962),
309–93. Most of the established facts about Marston's life derive
from Brettle's work.

CAMPBELL, O. J. *Comicall Satyre and Shakespeare's Troilus and Cressida.* San
Marino, Cal.: 1938. Vigorous but unconvincing argument that
Shakespeare's play is in the tradition of Marston's and Jonson's
satiric plays. The survey of this tradition is complete.

CAPUTI, ANTHONY. *John Marston, Satirist.* Ithaca, N. Y.: Cornell University Press, 1961. Argues the unity of thought behind the verse satires
and the plays; stresses the dominance of neo-stoicism in Marston's
thought. The sensible reminder that the plays were written to be
acted by boys leads, at times, to an overemphasis of the qualities of
parody and burlesque in them.

COLLEY, JOHN SCOTT. " 'Opinion' and the Reader in John Marston's *The
Metamorphosis of Pigmalion's Image,*" *English Literary Renaissance,* III

(Spring, 1973), 221–31. The poem "reveals how lovers, poets, and especially readers are overpowered by the forces of folly and self-deception"; the revelation is only partially successful, but Marston's grounds for defending his poem should be accepted even though he handles them awkwardly.

CROSS, GUSTAV. "Marston's 'Metamorphosis of Pigmalion's Image': A mock-epyllion," *Etudes Anglaises*, XIII (1960), 331–36. Argues it was a parody aimed at witty Inns of Court audience.

———. "Marston, Montaigne and Morality: *The Dutch Courtesan* Reconsidered," *English Literary History*, XXVII (1960), 30–43. Best short study of the play.

———. "Some Notes on the Vocabulary of John Marston," a series of twenty-four articles in *Notes and Queries* running from October, 1954 to August, 1963.

———. "The Authorship of 'Lust's Dominion,'" *Studies in Philology*, LV (1958), 38–61. Argues case for Marston on incidence of neologisms, parallels, themes, language, and personal reference.

———. "The Retrograde Genius of John Marston," *Review of English Literature*, II (October, 1961), 19–27. Stresses Marston's lasting concern with moral and philosophical problems; moves from a testing of the limitations of Stoicism to an appreciation of its adequacy in *Sophonisba*.

ELLIS-FERMOR, UNA. *The Jacobean Drama*. 4th Ed. London: Methuen, 1958. Best introduction to the subject. Her Appendix I "The Theatre War" is an excellent brief survey of opinion and writings.

FINKELPEARL, PHILIP J. "Donne and Everard Guilpin: Additions, Corrections, and Conjectures," *Review of English Studies*, XIV (1963), 164–67. Suggests relationship of Marston and Guilpin by marriage which Brettle later supports (see above).

———. "From Petrarch to Ovid: Metamorphoses in John Marston's 'Metamorphosis of Pigmalion's Image,'" *English Literary History*, XXXII (1965), 333–48. The poem has some serious elements but is actually satiric.

———. "Henry Walley of the Stationers' Company and John Marston," *Publications of Bibliographical Society of America*, LVI (1962), 366–68. Walley, sometime Master of Stationers' Company and a friend of Marston, possibly instrumental in dealing with Sheares and trouble over 1633 edition.

———. "John Marston's 'Histriomastix' as an Inns of Court Play: A Hypothesis," *Huntington Library Quarterly*, XXIX (1966), 223–34.

———. "Use of the Middle Temple's Christmas Revels in Marston's 'The Fawne,'" *Studies in Philology*, LXIV (1967), 199–209. Two convincingly argued articles connecting Marston's Inns of Court living with his plays.

———. *John Marston of the Middle Temple: An Elizabethan Dramatist in his*

Social Setting. Cambridge, Mass.: Harvard University Press, 1969. Surveys whole corpus of Marston against his Middle Temple background. Fine, perceptive study.

FOAKES, R. A. "John Marston's Fantastical Plays: 'Antonio and Mellida' and 'Antonio's Revenge,' " *Philological Quarterly,* XLI (1962), 229–38. Stresses perhaps too strongly the effect of children as actors and the general tendency of plays to use parodistic elements but an important, vigorous essay.

————. *Shakespeare the Dark Comedies to the Last Plays: From Satire to Celebration.* London: Routledge & Kegan Paul, 1971. Contains sections on "Jonson, Marston and satire" and satirical comedy, and on "Tragedy for boy-actors and tragedy for adult actors: Marston, Jonson, and Tourneur" which develop arguments for particular effects of boys' acting style; stresses comic-grotesque qualities of Marston.

FROST, DAVID. *The School of Shakespeare: The Influence of Shakespeare on English Drama 1600–42.* Cambridge: Cambridge University Press, 1968. Defensive study with the emphasis on Shakespeare as provider. His fellows appear largely as takers, pilferers, and thieves rather than as users, borrowers, or adapters of material. However, much old-fashioned gathering of verbal parallels is eschewed, and the influence is measured chiefly in themes, attitudes, and philosophies. The chapter on Revenge Tradition deals with Marston and argues for *Antonio's Revenge* as following *Hamlet.* Other connections between Marston and Shakespeare are only very glancingly mentioned.

GAIR, W. R. "La compagnie des enfants de St. Paul, Londres (1599–1606)." *Dramaturgie et Société, XVIᵉ et XVIIᵉ siècles.* Ed., Jean Jaquot. Paris: Editions du Centre National de la Recherche Scientifique, 1968. II, 655–74. Lively discussion of the War of the Theatres; an interesting stress upon the arguments about esthetics of writing and of acting.

GECKLE, GEORGE L. "Fortune in Marston's *The Malcontent,*" *Publications of the Modern Language Association,* LXXXVI (1971), 202–209. The Wheel of Fortune is the central structural and thematic symbol of the play's rising and falling pattern. This pattern is moral and Christian.

GIBBONS, BRIAN. *Jacobean City Comedy: A Study of Satiric Plays by Jonson, Marston and Middleton.* London: Hart-Davies, 1968. Uses social and economic background of period to illuminate the plays with a satisfying insistence upon their life as stage commentaries and not merely social history in dialogue form.

GILL, R. B. "A Purchase of Glory: The Persona of Late Elizabethan Satire," *Studies in Philology,* LXXII (1975), 408–18. The distinctions between the satirist and the persona need to be very carefully drawn in Hall, Guilpin, and Marston. The persona is used to display personal virtuosity. The two voices combine to represent the author as he would like to be seen in his role as satirist.

HARBAGE, ALFRED. *Shakespeare and the Rival Traditions.* New York:

Macmillan, 1952. Treats Marston with distaste and impugns his moral views with an almost Marstonian vigor. Nonetheless, valuable study of the different tastes of private and public theaters.

HARRIS, BERNARD. "Dissent and Satire," *Shakespeare Survey*, XVII (1964), 120–37.

————. "Men Like Satyres." *Elizabethan Poetry*. Edited by J. R. Brown and B. Harris. Stratford Upon Avon Studies, II. London: Edward Arnold, 1960. pp. 175–201. Two excellent general surveys of Elizabethan satire.

HIGGINS, M. "The Convention of the Stoic Hero as Handled by Marston," *Modern Language Review*, XXXIX (1943), pp. 338–46. Discusses Marston's fusing of Revenger and Stoic in one figure. Very useful article.

HUNTER, GEORGE K. "English Folly and Italian Vice: The Moral Landscape of John Marston," *Jacobean Theatre*. Edited by J. R. Brown and B. Harris. Stratford Upon Avon Studies, I. London: Edward Arnold, 1960. pp. 85–112. Examines underlying moral concern in Marston's plays as expressed in the pull between the conventions of the plot and the stage; Marston's own moral interests; the kind of Italianate setting he chose and the way he handled it.

INGRAM, R. W. "The Use of Music in the Plays of Marston," *Music and Letters*, XXXVII (1956), 154–64. Surveys plays generally but deals especially with *Sophonisba*, the two parts of *Antonio and Mellida*, conventions of large-scale dance and inter-act music.

JENSEN, EINER. "Theme and Imagery in *The Malcontent*," *Studies in English Literature*, X (1970), 367–84. Pattern of imagery centers on rise and fall in the court with fable of tortoise and eagle the focus of similarly patterned animal imagery.

KAPLAN, JOEL. "John Marston's *Fawn*: A Saturnalian Satire," *Studies in English Literature*, IX (1969), 335–50. "A Saturnalian satire in which a process of suppling replaces the satirist's more traditional lancet and invective is superseded by a rhetoric of increase."

KEACH, WILLIAM. *Elizabethan Erotic Narratives: Irony and Pathos in the Ovidian Poetry of Shakespeare, Marlowe, and Their Contemporaries.* New Brunswick, N.J.: Rutgers University Press, 1977. *Pigmalion's Image* is a "highly self-conscious and unevenly written exercise in Ovidian narrative poetry."

KERNAN, ALVIN. *The Cankered Muse: Satire of the English Renaissance.* New Haven: Yale University Press, 1959. Exciting book which applies to Renaissance satire some of the approaches familiar from studies of Augustan and later satire. Directs attention to the principle of relating the satire to the goal rather than to the satirist. Distinction between the author and his satiric persona is stressed.

KIEFER, CHRISTIAN. "Music and Marston's 'The Malcontent,' " *Studies in Philology*, LI (1954), 163–71. Useful gathering of standard Elizabethan feelings about music applied to music in the play.

KIRSCH, ARTHUR C. *Jacobean Dramatic Perspectives*. Charlottesville: University Press of Virginia, 1972. Traces influence of rise of satirical comedy, tragicomedy, and the private theater on changes in dramatic taste in Jacobean England. Concise and excellent.

LECOCQ, LOUIS. "Travaux récents sur John Marston," *Etudes Anglaises*, XVI (1963), 351–63. Excellent review article.

LYONS, BRIDGET G. *Voices of Melancholy: Studies in Literary Treatments of Melancholy in Renaissance England*. London: Routledge & Kegan Paul, 1971. The third chapter, "Marston and Melancholy" (pp. 58–76) marks Marston's fascination with melancholy and its literary possibilities; Lampatho Doria, Antonio, Feliche, and Malevole are especially dealt with. A sensible survey of the topic.

MEHL, DIETER. *The Elizabethan Dumb Show: The History of a Dramatic Convention*. London: Methuen, 1965. Standard history. Chapter 8, pp. 123–37, deals with Marston.

O'NEILL, DAVID G. "The Commencement of Marston's Career as a Dramatist," *Review of English Studies*, ns LXXXVIII (1971), 442–45. Reports alteration by John Marston, Sr. in his will concerning his son's playwriting.

————. "The Influence of Music in the Works of John Marston," *Music and Letters*, LIII (1972), 122–33, 293–308, 400–410. Illustrates "the breadth and scope of Marston's knowledge and employment of musical terminology." Argues for rich and sensitive use of musical terms and ideas comparable with Shakespeare's (in my own researches on this topic, I rank Marston, Fletcher, and Brome with Shakespeare as the most consistently sensitive and frequent users of musical terms and music in their plays).

ORNSTEIN, ROBERT. *The Moral Vision of Jacobean Tragedy*. Madison: University of Wisconsin Press, 1960. Excellent book that stimulates enthusiasm and discussion. "Those with a taste for the intellectual gossip of the Jacobean literary world might spend a few profitable though not very edifying hours in [Marston's] company" (163).

PETER, JOHN. *Complaint and Satire in Early English Literature*. Oxford: Clarendon Press, 1956. Important study: deals with Marston as satirist rather than dramatist; takes a generally disapproving attitude toward him.

PRESSON, ROBERT. "Marston's 'Dutch Courtesan': The Study of an Attitude in Adaptation," *Journal of English and Germanic Philology*, LV (1956), 406–13. Interesting source study.

SCHOENBAUM, SAMUEL. "The Precarious Balance of Marston," *Publications of the Modern Language Association*, LXVII (1952), 1069–78. Stresses the wilder aspects of Marston, but a standard expression of one opinion held about Marston.

SHAPIRO, MICHAEL. *Children of the Revels: The Boy Companies of*

Shakespeare's Time and Their Plays. New York: Columbia University Press, 1977. Standard survey of this topic: considerable reference to Marston throughout.

SLIGHTS, WILLIAM W. E. " 'Elder in a deform'd church': The Function of Marston's Malcontent," *Studies in English Literature,* XIII (Spring, 1973), 360–73. Marston combines satiric exposure and comic pattern of regeneration to cleanse court and its central characters (it also is self-educating experience for Altofronto).

SPENCER, THEODORE. "John Marston," *Criterion,* XIII (1934), 581–99. Best single essay on Marston; covers all aspects of his work. Suggestive comments on his poetic art.

SPENS, JANET. *Shakespeare's Relation to Tradition.* Oxford: H. Blackwell, 1916. Neglected little book: takes up relationship of *Antonio's Revenge* to *Hamlet* and *Macbeth.*

STEIN, ARNOLD. "Donne's Harshness and the Elizabethan tradition," *Studies in Philology,* XLI (1944), 390–409.

———. "Donne and the Satiric Spirit," *English Literary History,* XI (1944), 266–82.

———. "Donne's Obscurity and the Elizabethan Tradition," *ibid.,* XIII (1946), 98–118.

———. "The Second English Satirist," *Modern Language Review,* XXXVIII (1943), 273–78. Very good articles on some of the traditions of Elizabethan verse satire within which Marston worked.

STILLING, ROGER. *Love and Death in Renaissance Tragedy.* Baton Rouge: Louisiana State University Press, 1976. Chapter 6, "Antonio and Mellida: I & II," pp. 82–96, Argues that satire in plays is rooted in their context of romantic tragedies: the object of the satire is courtly love and courtly flirtation which debase the ideal of romantic marriage.

STOLL, E. E. "Shakespeare, Marston and the Malcontent Type," *Modern Philology,* III (1906), 281–303. Old but characteristically trenchant, and useful.

SWINBURNE, ALGERNON. *The Age of Shakespeare.* London, 1908. The most neglected major English dramatic critic. His surging style cannot obscure the general interest and frequent power of his observations. The study of Marston shows him at his most charactertistic. His dismissal of *Histriomastix* from consideration is especially flamboyant.

THORNDIKE, A. "The Relation of 'Hamlet' to Contemporary Revenge Plays," *Publications of Modern Language Association,* XVII (1902), 125–220. Marston is discussed on pp. 155–168.

URE, P. "Marston's 'Sophonisba': A Reconsideration," *Durham University Journal,* N.S. X (1949), 81–90. Particularly good on the thought of the play.

WEISS, ADRIEN. "Rhetoric and Satire: New Light on John Marston's *Pigmalion* and the Satires," *Journal of English and Germanic Philology,* LXXI (1972), 22–35. *Pigmalion* is part and parcel of the satires: it is a product of the persona who is Kinsayder. He is the "object of satire in regard to his performance in *Pigmalion* and the satires, and that in delineating Kinsayder, Marston defines the pitfalls of self-deception due to pride, especially in regard to the poet who assumes a satiric stance without first coming to an adequate knowledge of self."

Index

178